AMANDA MEJIAS

THIS IS
GIRLS
MINISTRY

YOUR RELATIONAL STRATEGY TO REACH TEEN GIRLS

Published by Lifeway Press® • © 2023
Reprinted Oct. 2023

ISBN: 978-1-0877-6758-1
Item: 005838176
Dewey decimal classification: 259.23
Subject heading: GIRLS \ TEENAGERS \ CHURCH WORK WITH TEENAGE GIRLS

Editorial Team, Lifeway Girls Bible Studies

BEN TRUEBLOOD
Director,
Lifeway Students

JOHN PAUL BASHAM
Manager, Student
Publishing

KAREN DANIEL
Team Leader

MORGAN HAWK
Content Editor

JENNIFER SIAO
Production Editor

STEPHANIE SALVATORE
Graphic Designer

To order additional copies of this resource, write Lifeway Resources Customer Service; 200 Powell Place, Suite 100, Brentwood, TN 37027; Fax order to 615.251.5933; call toll-free 800.458.2772; email orderentry@lifeway.com; or order online at lifeway.com.

Printed in the United States of America.

Lifeway Girls
Lifeway Resources
200 Powell Place, Suite 100
Brentwood, TN 37027

Amanda Mejias serves as the Lifeway

Girls Brand Specialist, which is just a super fun way
of saying that she serves the parents and leaders
of teen girls. After serving on church staff for many
years, she is passionate about building relationships
and creating resources that equip the local church.
Amanda is wife to her wonderful husband, Brandon,
and lives out her dream of being a working mom. If
you ever want to find a way to her heart, ask to meet
for coffee or send her a TikTok of a golden retriever.

TO KARIS:
YOU'RE SO
MUCH MORE
THAN A STORY
I GET TO
SHARE, BUT I
AM HONORED
TO SHARE
WITH THE
WORLD HOW
MUCH YOU
IMPACTED
MY LIFE AND
THE WAY YOU
CHANGED
GIRLS
MINISTRY
FOREVER.

Table of Contents

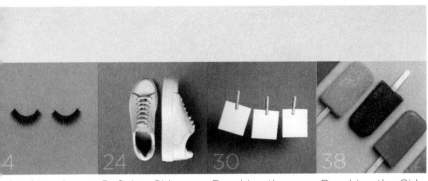

PART 1

THE PURPOSE IT HAS:

A PINK SPRINKLE DONUT

Growing up I had a thing against birthday cakes. I don't know why I thought all cakes were gross or inedible, but I could not comprehend why cake was the dessert of choice for so many people on their birthdays. While my taste buds have since matured and I'd take a piece of chocolate cake over just about anything, I have always gravitated toward donuts. Anyone who has known me for any length of time knows this. I *love* donuts.

I love a good, hot donut that is rolled in cinnamon sugar, but one of my favorites is a plain, chocolate-iced from a local shop in Nashville. Growing up, however, I was "donut-sheltered" and only had access to a few places like Krispy Kreme and Dunkin' Donuts. So every year on my birthday, I requested the same donut as my celebration treat.

A pink sprinkle donut from Dunkin' Donuts.

I still crave that donut whenever I think about it, but it never quite hits the spot quite like it did when I was twelve. However, that pink sprinkle donut now represents far more than birthday celebrations or childhood memories. It represents what I have come to know and love as girls ministry.

In August of 2013, I began a full-time position at my church working with a small team to launch a multi-site campus. We didn't have a building or offices on that first day, but I remember walking into a room of cubicles and getting to meet Rebecca for the first time. This preschool director and complete stranger would soon become one of my lifelong best friends and matron of honor in my wedding. I could write a second book about all the ways she has changed my life and how so many of my ministry lessons were taught by and learned alongside Rebecca.

When you launch a church or campus with a small group of people, you instantly become family. You're around each other *all* the time doing *all* the things that no one ever sees but are one hundred percent necessary and required to make things happen. This is where I got to know Rebecca and her family.

Rebecca and her husband, John, have three hilarious, loving, and beautiful kids—Rendon, Aliya, and Karis. We won't talk about the fact that they're all high school graduates because that will just make me feel old. All three of them are so incredibly special to me; however, we're going to focus on Karis because she plays an important role in the pink sprinkle donut story that will completely change how you view girls ministry. At least, that's what happened for me.

Karis was only eight years old when I met her. A spunky fourth grader who could make you laugh or cry depending on her level of sarcasm that day, but she was an absolute blast to be around. Growing up with a parent in full-time ministry, she understood what it meant to serve and love others well—even if it was in her own Karis kind of way. (We try not to remind her of the times when she would bite and kick her small group leaders, but it was definitely her way of saying that she was secretly a big fan of you.)

Karis had (and still does) a way of reading people and determining whether or not she could trust them. Even at a young age, she wanted people to respect and validate her. Karis didn't want to be treated like a little kid or "the preschool director's daughter," but she also didn't want people digging into her emotional or personal bubble because that would be a little too close for comfort. However, even at the age of eight, I believed that she would become the kind of Jesus follower who would change the world.

After several months spent getting to know Karis, I realized that like most pre-teen and teen girls, it was going to take more than a few conversations before she was ready to trust or confide in me. I can't tell you the first time Karis and I really clicked, but I do know it was a gradual process. It was hours of setting up kids ministry baskets together for her mom, going on Walmart runs, and grabbing Mexican for lunch after church each Sunday with her family.

I always looked for points of connection to help Karis know I loved and cared for her. And one day, I discovered we had a mutual love for something that would continue to help me find ways to intentionally build a relationship with her for years to come.

THIS PICTURE IS FROM A SUNDAY MORNING IN JULY 2014—OUR FIRST OF MANY PINK SPRINKLE DONUTS.

A pink sprinkle donut from Dunkin' Donuts.

I don't remember when we discovered our similar affection for this subpar donut, but if you've ever worked at or attended church, you know donuts often find their way into ministry spaces. So every time I went to grab donuts for an event or passed by Dunkin' Donuts on an errand, I would always grab two extra pink sprinkle donuts for Karis and me.

Now let's fast-forward to 2016. After one year of marriage, my husband and I brought home our first baby: a Golden Retriever puppy named Coda. When you and your husband both work in ministry full-time, taking care of a puppy can get tricky, but 10/10 recommend getting a Golden Retriever. Wednesdays were my longest days—often at church until after 8 p.m., then grabbing a late night dinner with staff and students. That meant before student and kids activities began, I had to drive home to check on Coda.

One Wednesday, I extended the invitation to Karis to ride along with me. A puppy probably would've been enough motivation, but I threw in an extra bonus: "We can grab a sprinkle donut from Dunkin' after, if you want?" Karis was in!

For the next three years of the regular Wednesday night marathons, that is exactly what we did (as long as Karis had finished her homework). We didn't always get donuts. Sometimes, it was coffee or frozen yogurt, or we had just enough time to let Coda out and race back before programming began. But those Wednesday drives with Karis are some of my favorite memories.

It was during those drives that we connected and laughed and created our own inside jokes, but we also talked through the deep stuff. I always wanted Karis to know I cared about how she was really doing and who she was hanging out with. I tried really hard (probably sometimes too hard) to make her feel safe venting, asking questions, or just being real. And in return, I was always real with her.

Friends, *this is girls ministry*.

It wasn't some fancy event or manipulated way of getting Karis to spend time with me. It wasn't a fancy Bible study or a lecture about purity. It was just a simple invitation into my regular space and routine where I could give her a place to feel known, loved, and safe. The pink sprinkle donut wasn't the end-all, be-all of how I connected with Karis. It was just the method God used in that season for me to start building a relationship with her.

Whoever you are, God has provided your own pink sprinkle donut strategy for girls ministry. And let me just say, it's probably not an event or a mother-daughter weekend away or another sermon. While God can and will use those things to disciple and lead teen girls to Christ, the girls ministry strategy that I hope you will discover through this book is relational.

Imagine Jesus only ever preaching the Sermon on the Mount to His disciples but never actually spending time with them. Do you think the disciples would ever believe anything He taught without witnessing firsthand the miracles or the love and compassion Jesus had for them?

Teen girls need to hear the truth, but they also need to watch how other Jesus followers live faithfully and love others well. They need safe places to be vulnerable and wrestle with hard questions. They need to know that you don't just want to preach at them or "change them," but that you love them unconditionally and truly want them to know and experience God's love. You can give one-hundred lectures or teach the best sermons of your life, but if you miss the relational aspect of discipleship, you will not reach the teen girls in your life.

And yes, this absolutely looks different for everyone. How a mom or dad has a relationship with their daughter will and should look differently from how a student pastor has a relationship with the teen girls in his ministry. And how a girls minister builds relationships with teen girls will look different from a soccer coach or grandma. But each of us has been equipped by God to play a role in girls ministry with unique stories, gifts, and personalities. This kind of girls ministry doesn't require anything fancy or expensive, and you most likely won't need a pink sprinkle donut for it. But it does require an obedient heart.

THE ONLY PICTURE I HAVE TO REMEMBER OUR WEEKLY CAR RIDES.

My prayer is that this book will open your eyes to see how God has formed you uniquely in this season of life to reach teen girls for the sake of the gospel and His glory. I encourage you to put away any preconceived notions that you might have about teen girls or girls ministry in general as you read. May you read with open hands and willing feet to do whatever it takes to help teen girls feel known, loved, and seen by their God.

But before we move on, I want to clarify an important purpose of this book that is often unpopular and can cause confusion when assumptions are made about girls ministry.

There are numerous events I've attended while working for Lifeway where we set up a Lifeway Girls and Lifeway Students table to show off the resources that we are working on to better serve church leaders. It has happened more often than it should that someone begins questioning why we even offer something for Lifeway Girls.

I can always feel the questions coming as I watch them glance through the resources on the tables, while dropping lots of "hmms" as they not-so-quietly whisper to themselves. Finally, when they make eye contact with me, they'll say in a half-joking tone, "So, I see you have Lifeway Girls, but why is there no Lifeway Teen Guys?"

I mean, it's a fair question.

Why do we have more girls-only resources? Why do I need to write a book about discipling and reaching teen girls? Why is girls ministry needed when there isn't a guys ministry in most churches?

First of all, it has absolutely nothing to do with valuing teen girls over teen guys. Nothing you read in this book will say guys ministry isn't important, and you will not find a single sentence in this book telling you to prioritize ministering to teen girls over teen guys. Parents are called just as much to disciple their teen sons as they are to disciple their daughters.

Teen girls and teen guys are both created equal in the image of God (Gen. 1:26-27). However, while equal, guys and girls are also designed differently with unique gifts, desires, and needs. And when churches and student ministries are often more male-led, the unique needs of a teen girl can easily be overlooked or undervalued (and just plain scary to some). Therefore, we must honor and steward the emotional, physical, and mental differences God created.

This doesn't mean that the topics we talk about with teen girls, the Scripture that we study, or the goals of discipleship that we create will be any different than what we are called to do for teen guys. But throughout this book, you will learn how to take what you might do for all teens and mold it in such a way that will better relate to your teen girls.

I am praying that as you read each chapter, the Lord will give you eyes to see teen girls the same way He does. I pray He will soften your heart toward meeting girls where they are versus asking them to be something they're not. I pray that you will surrender any false versions of teen girl discipleship and that you will lean into how God might want to use you in the lives of the teen girls around you.

WHEN CHURCHES AND STUDENT MINISTRIES ARE OFTEN MORE MALE-LED, THE UNIQUE NEEDS OF A TEEN GIRL CAN EASILY BE OVERLOOKED.

DEBUNKING
THE

YOU DON'T HAVE TO LIKE CRAFTS OR
PAINTING NAILS . . . OR OWN A SINGLE
PINK THING TO DO GIRLS MINISTRY. YOU
CAN TEACH GIRLS THE WHOLE BIBLE
WITHOUT GIVING CHEESY ILLUSTRATIONS
INVOLVING FLOWERS AND TEA PARTIES.

CHAPTER 1

MYTHS OF GIRLS MINISTRY

I've talked to countless pastors, girls ministers, and parents about how they would define girls ministry. Almost every person would agree and acknowledge that girls ministry involves ministering to and discipling teen girls. What almost every person would disagree with is how that actually looks. While I would agree that girls ministry will look different for every single person in every single context, there are some general myths about girls ministry that are just wrong. I want to break down some of those misconceptions about girls ministry in order to help set a more accurate foundation of what girls ministry is and what it is not.

MYTH #1: GIRLS MINISTRY IS FOR "GIRLY" THINGS.

When I began thinking through the cover of this book, I only knew two things I did *not* want on the front: flowers and anything pink. As a girl who hates shopping and spends about five minutes getting ready every day, I am not the poster child for "girly girl." Never in a million years did I think someone would hire me to do girls ministry—let alone write a book on it. But here I am in my neutrals and Nike high-tops, please still love me.

While I think culture has gotten a lot of things wrong about what is defined as "girly," I believe the church has missed it for decades. You can probably name a few girls ministry events that you've been to or heard of, as well as resources specifically designed for girls. Let me guess some of the topics you've covered:

- Find Beauty Within
- You Are a Princess of God
- Modesty Is Hottest-y
- Purity Rocks!

I'm cracking up even as I write these topics because I know you've heard of these things too. You may have even hosted an event with one of these themes. And honestly, that's okay. I'm not here to say we shouldn't talk about a girl's self-image or God's design for sex. We should and need to talk about those things with teen girls. They're asking us for conversations like that.

But want to know a little secret? Girls ministry involves the entire scope of Scripture—not just the cultural issues we want to address with teen girls or our made-up interpretation of the Proverbs 31 woman.

This myth of girls ministry is one of the biggest barriers I have seen in building effective discipleship with teen girls. We cannot and will not do girls ministry if we are only focusing on identity or telling girls not to wear two-piece bathing suits.

Girls ministry must include showing girls how to study the Bible and how to live out the gospel. Girls ministry needs to include the teaching of both men and women in Scripture. Girls ministry should help girls learn to be better friends and to discover what repentance actually looks like.

And you know what else? You don't have to like crafts or painting nails. You don't even have to know how to make a charcuterie board or own a single pink thing to do girls ministry. You can teach girls the whole Bible without giving cheesy illustrations involving flowers and tea parties.

I hope this offers many of you, like me, a sigh of relief. You don't have to be classified as girly to do girls ministry. And for the rest of you who love pink and sparkles, that's more than okay. God created you to reach girls with your girly self and to create the most beautiful events and have endless chats with girls about their self-worth. Just don't stop there! Girls want and need more. We all have such an important role in girls ministry.

Girls ministry is not just about purity, beauty, or modesty. If you want to teach teen girls what it means to be "girly" as a follower of Jesus, show them what it looks like to take up their crosses and lay down their lives to follow Him.

MYTH #2: GIRLS MINISTRY IS RESERVED FOR GIRLS MINISTERS.

There is a GroupMe text of almost one hundred girls ministers that I was added to when I first started my role as the Girls Brand Specialist at Lifeway. I have never been more obsessed with or intimidated by a group of women in my entire life. These women are incredible followers of Jesus, and they are stellar at ministering to and discipling teen girls in their ministry, in addition to all the other duties that come with working in student ministry (IYKYK).

But do you want to know what issue I see these women face almost every day in their ministry? They have been given the sole responsibility of discipling every single teen girl in the ministry. Most of these women work at larger churches with student ministries ranging from fifty to one thousand students. Can you imagine the weight of being handed a list of 25, 50, 75, or 500 teen girls and saying, "These girls are your responsibility. Do whatever it takes to care for their souls. Oh, and you may or may not have a budget to do so."

Yea, it's no wonder why so many of them feel isolated or burnt out. It's a lot for any one person to shoulder. Let me correct that. It's impossible for any one person. (And all my girls ministers say, amen!)

IF YOU WANT TO TEACH TEEN GIRLS WHAT IT MEANS TO BE "GIRLY" AS A FOLLOWER OF JESUS, SHOW THEM WHAT IT LOOKS LIKE TO TAKE UP THEIR CROSSES AND LAY DOWN THEIR LIVES TO FOLLOW HIM.

YOU DON'T
NEED A GIRLS
MINISTER. YOU
DON'T EVEN
NEED A BUDGET.
THOSE THINGS
ARE INCREDIBLY
LIFE-GIVING
TO THE TEEN
GIRLS UNDER
YOUR SCOPE OF
INFLUENCE, BUT
GIRLS MINISTRY
IS SO MUCH
MORE THAN
THE PEOPLE
YOUR CHURCH
EMPLOYS. WE
NEED THEM,
BUT WE ALSO
NEED YOU.

I know that one-hundred girls ministers sounds like a lot at first. I mean these women are truly outstanding and pour out their lives to minister to the teen girls God has entrusted them with. But when we scale back and see the number of churches and teen girls that exist inside the United States alone, this number is teeny tiny. If the whole premise of girls ministry rests on these hundred women alone, we have failed as the body of Christ to reach teen girls effectively.

Most likely, you're reading this book because you don't have a girls minister at your church, and you're wondering how in the world you and your church can do a better job ministering to teen girls. Let me encourage you by saying that you don't need a girls minister. You don't even need a budget.

Those things are incredibly life-giving to the teen girls within your circle of influence, but girls ministry is so much more than the people your church employs. We need them, but we also need you.

If you do have a girls minister at your church, know that you are so incredible blessed to have that kind of leadership in your student ministry. It truly is a rare gift inside the church. Make sure to thank her and show her how much she is valued. This might include making sure she is paid well, has opportunities to grow as a leader, and has the full support of her church family.

And as you continue to read this book and discover how you can intentionally disciple teen girls, please know that the greatest gift you can give to any girls minister is to faithfully live out your role in girls ministry.

MYTH #3: GIRLS MINISTRY IS NOT FOR MEN.

One of the first training events that I led for Lifeway as the Girls Brand Specialist was for a group of student ministers. I was tasked with presenting a quick training and overview of what girls ministry is and how this group played a role in girls ministry. At this point, my own view of girls ministry was still skewed, and I was really trying to figure out how I even ended up in this position. But here I was, standing in front of a room full of student ministers that were primarily male and giving my best speech on girls ministry.

I taught them why discipling teen girls is unique and important. I shared how they could find room in their budget to offer girls-only events at their churches. I explained the importance of setting up female leaders from the church to disciple, and I even made a joke about how student ministers shouldn't take girls out for coffee so find someone who can. Overall, it felt like a good first attempt at a girls ministry training.

Zac Workun, the training specialist who hosted the event, came by my desk later that day to check in on how I was feeling after. I thought it was okay overall, but I asked him for some feedback since it was my first time. Zac is now one of my good friends and someone I seek for ministry advice often, but at that point, I didn't know him very well and had no idea that he was the kind of person who wouldn't hold back from the truth.

Zac graciously told me, "You gave them lots of good tips and tricks on getting girls ministry going and recruiting leaders. But what about all the things they can do as male student pastors to disciple teen girls?"

I didn't like his answer. (Sorry, Zac!) I was honestly irritated after he walked away. He's a guy, so what does he know about girls ministry? I mean, male student ministers shouldn't go get coffee with a girl or send encouraging texts to girls throughout the week. Men shouldn't be having one-on-one conversations with girls. How could they disciple teen girls without those things?

I wrestled with his feedback for a few weeks. I felt like Rehoboam going to my friends for advice on something I probably already knew how to handle (see 1 Kings 12). But I just couldn't get past what I did know about girls ministry.

So I'd ask friends, "Should I actually listen to Zac?" "He's not right, right?" "That's just unwise advice!" I was looking for someone to affirm how I felt about girls ministry, but, instead, I found myself uncovering layers of girls ministry that I didn't know existed.

One of the conversations that helped shift my perspective was with my friend and boss, John Paul. John Paul was a student pastor for many years and was someone I trusted to speak truth over the situation. Instead of giving me what I wanted to hear, John Paul shared his own stories and struggles of discipling teen girls as a student pastor. He told me that one of his regrets as a student pastor was his lack of intentionality in ministering to teen girls. (I'm going to share more of his story in Chapter Six for the faithful men in ministry reading this book.)

I was really humbled that day by my conversation with John Paul, and I tell Zac all the time how much he impacted my entire outlook on girls ministry. Because after both of these godly men lovingly challenged me to invite men into girls ministry, I began to see the many ways that men played an important role in my own story of discipleship.

It was my male student pastors in high school who developed my love of theology and the study of God's Word. It was the husbands of my small group leaders who were incredible examples of love, service, and fun. It was my best friend's dad who helped me find my first car, taught me how to change my oil, and introduced me to the art of the potato gun. It was my uncle who would give me driving lessons, talk for hours about life and ministry, and then walk me down the aisle one day.

These are just a few examples of how men played a significant role in ministering to me as a teen girl. I can honestly say that I would not be the same person without them. I needed those men in my life (and I still do), and I know that every single teen girl today needs men just like them as examples of godliness, strength, and fun.

In case you haven't heard this before, let me say it for you loud and clear:

Men have a place in girls ministry.

Men can be girls ministers.

We need men in girls ministry.

MYTH #4: GIRLS MINISTRY ISN'T FOR ME.

I've addressed three of the excuses I hear about why people don't think girls ministry has anything to do with them. But if you aren't someone who thinks you have to be more girly, or a girls minister, or a woman to do girls ministry, I want to know, what's your excuse?

What's holding you back from discovering the role God has given you in discipling and ministering to the teen girls that He has entrusted to you? Is it one of these excuses?

- I don't have enough time in my schedule to add anything else.
- I don't know how to teach girls the Bible.
- I don't know how to relate to teen girls.
- I don't know many teen girls.
- I don't want them to know my mistakes from when I was a teen.
- I don't want them to see how I'm struggling.
- I don't even like talking to teen girls.
- I don't have it all together.

To be honest, I have used almost every single one of those excuses in my own life. I have come up with all the reasons I think someone else should be leading that particular small group, or talking to a girl about her struggles, or inviting girls into her home. My life is messy most days. I am far from having it all together, and I have never felt more out of place than when an eighth-grade girl is telling me about her love for *Dungeons and Dragons*.

On my way to church on Sunday to lead my small group, I'll often pray something like, "God, use someone else. You've got the wrong person for this. I can't do it. I don't want to do it."

It's then that I remember Exodus 3, when God reveals Himself to Moses at the burning bush. After God tells Moses that He wants to use him to free the Israelites from Egyptian slavery, Moses says, "Who am I?" (v. 11), a.k.a. "Wow, God, cool offer. I think that's great, but I am pretty sure you've got the wrong guy!"

Kind of sounds like the prayer I pray to Him before meeting with my girls. But I love how God doesn't respond to Moses with the list of qualifications that make Moses awesome for the job. He doesn't say, "Well, Moses, you have all this free time, and you've met all My requirements to tell Pharaoh to let My people go. So I just know you will do great!" Instead, God says, "I will certainly be with you" (v. 12), and "I AM WHO AM" (v. 14).

It had nothing to do with Moses. It had everything to do with God.

I want to encourage you to not believe the myth that Moses believed about being the wrong person for God's calling. You might be thinking there is no reason for God to use you to disciple teen girls. You might be thinking that this could not come at a worse time for God to be asking you to do anything else. You might think that you are the least qualified, but here's what you have to know:

Girls ministry is not about you.

But girls ministry is for you. Because the God who has called you to make disciples of every nation is for you, He goes before you, and He will be with you wherever you may go.

Because of who God is, He can use every spare minute and broken piece of your life for the sake of discipling teen girls. He isn't seeking perfection or even people who look like they have it all together. He is just looking for someone to surrender to His call to obey.

GIRLS MINISTRY IS NOT ABOUT YOU. BUT GIRLS MINISTRY IS FOR YOU.

ELLIE & CAROLINE

In December 2020, my student pastor asked me to disciple two girls, Ellie and Caroline, so we scheduled a coffee meetup. I loaded up my two-year old, which if you're a parent, you know is a whole thing. We were finally driving that way when my car's transmission unexpectedly went out.

Perfect. This has to be a sign that God definitely has the wrong person to disciple these teen girls.

I sent a text to Ellie and Caroline to fill them in on my situation, and I told them I'd be in touch when or if I could meet again. And that's when I discovered that these girls were exactly who I needed. They immediately responded, "I'm so sorry! We are coming to you right now and bringing you and Blakely Chick-fil-A!"

Those two girls who were strangers when we ate Chick-fil-A on my living room floor in 2020 are now like family. God used them to show me that it wasn't how they needed me, but how I needed them.

Girls ministry isn't just about what God can do through you; it's what God can do in you because of your teen girls.

DEFINING

AT THE BEGINNING OF JESUS'S COMMAND, HE SAYS, "GO." IT MEANS WHEREVER LIFE HAS YOU AND WHATEVER SEASON YOU FIND YOURSELF IN, YOU CAN MAKE DISCIPLES.

CHAPTER 2

GIRLS MINISTRY

The goal of girls ministry is to empower and equip girls to follow Jesus for the long haul. We don't just want teen girls to show up to church on Sundays or know a few Bible verses. We don't need more great rule followers in our ministries or in our homes. We don't want girls to know how to "talk the talk" without living out the fruit of their salvation. We don't want them to just hear the gospel, yet never share it.

No, we want disciples. We want teen girls to know God's Word and love it. We want them to be equipped to be who God has made them to be. We want them to feel empowered to share their testimonies and stand up for truth. We want them to not only be discipled but to be disciple makers. Because this is not just about teen girls today; it's about the women they will become in their twenties, forties, sixties, and beyond.

Therefore, we must start with the basic fundamentals of discipleship. Girls ministry at its core is discipleship, so let's see how Jesus set the foundation to effectively disciple teen girls.

LET'S TALK DISCIPLESHIP

The Great Commission is one of the last sermons Jesus preached to His disciples before ascending to heaven. You might even be familiar with His words in Matthew 28:19-20:

> "Go, therefore, and make disciples of all nations, baptizing them in the name of the Father and of the Son and of the Holy Spirit, teaching them to observe everything I have commanded you. And remember, I am with you always, to the end of the age."

Jesus commanded His disciples to go and make disciples of all nations. Sounds like a lot of responsibility for just eleven guys, right?

However, Jesus wasn't just giving a command to those eleven men who stood on the mountain with Him that day in Galilee. Those disciples would become His "witnesses in Jerusalem, in all Judea and Samaria, and to the ends of the earth" (Acts 1:8), but our call as Christ-followers remains the same as theirs. We are to make disciples.

But what does it mean to make disciples? Do we have to be qualified to disciple someone? Are there only certain points in our lives when discipleship applies to us? Let's break those questions down.

WHAT DOES IT MEAN TO MAKE DISCIPLES?

As a rabbi, Jesus chose His disciples to follow Him (literally). They learned firsthand all about Jesus—how He taught, spoke with people, ministered, performed miracles, and more. They didn't just stand back and watch from a distance. The disciples had hands-on experience and were in a real relationship with the One who had called them.

Jesus displayed the perfect example of discipleship for us to follow. Like Jesus, we're to invite people into our lives to see up close and personal what it means to follow Him. This begins with the gospel and baptism, but must be followed by teaching them everything we find in Scripture..

WE'RE TO INVITE PEOPLE INTO OUR LIVES TO SEE UP CLOSE AND PERSONAL WHAT IT MEANS TO FOLLOW HIM.

Jesus didn't do this by sitting in a circle with His disciples once a week to open the Law and answer discussion questions. Jesus taught His disciples through the way He lived. Yes, there were many sermons, but Jesus didn't just teach about prayer. He showed them what prayer looked like. He didn't just talk about how to care for their neighbors; He showed them what it looked like to serve others. He didn't just preach about giving; He showed them what it looked like to sacrifice His life.

Discipleship is our call to bring people alongside us to show them what it means to follow Jesus.

WHAT ARE THE QUALIFICATIONS FOR DISCIPLESHIP?

If you do a deep dive into the life and background of the disciples, you will know that Jesus didn't choose them because they were super qualified. These men weren't the smartest, most well-behaved, or perfectly religious. They would misunderstand Jesus, deny Him, and be rebuked by Him. Yet Jesus still chose these imperfect men to learn firsthand what it means to follow Him.

In Matthew 16:24-25, Jesus gave the most basic explanation of the qualifications needed to follow and be like Him.

> Then Jesus said to his disciples, "If anyone wants to follow after me, let him deny himself, take up his cross, and follow me. For whoever wants to save his life will lose it, but whoever loses his life because of me will find it."

Do you want to make disciples? Take up your cross and follow Him.

Do you want to make disciples? Deny yourself.

Do you want to make disciples? Find your life in Him.

Those are the only qualifications to start making disciples. Now ask yourself, what is holding you back from getting started?

WHEN IS DISCIPLESHIP EFFECTIVE?

At the beginning of Jesus's command, He says, "Go" (Matt. 28:19). According to the Blue Letter Bible, that one syllable word can be defined as "to pursue the journey on which one has entered, to continue on one's journey."[1] It does not say to make disciples when you've finally mastered theology, or have your kids out of the house, or when you are less busy at work. It means wherever life has you and in whatever season you find yourself, you can make disciples.

It's hard to imagine adding anything else to our plates, but that's when we forget that discipleship has nothing to do with our ability and everything to do with the power of the Holy Spirit. When Jesus told the disciples that they would be His witnesses in Acts 1:8, it was because they would have the power of the Holy Spirit. The same goes for us.

We can't change anyone's heart or even disciple someone apart from the work of the Holy Spirit. Therefore, it doesn't matter what our lives or seasons looks like. We can always be effective disciple makers because the Holy Spirit lives inside of us.

This should be such an encouragement to us! We don't need to get our lives together before making disciples or find the "right" way to do it. Effective discipleship is our full reliance on the Holy Spirit and complete surrender to the truth that Jesus is with us "always, to the end of the age" (Matt. 28:20b).

One of the most popular Bible verses on evangelism and discipleship comes from Acts 1:8, when Jesus is commissioning His disciples to be His witnesses. It says, "But you will receive power when the Holy Spirit has come on you, and you will be my witnesses in Jerusalem, in all Judea and Samaria, and to the ends of the earth."

But what does it mean to be a witness? Is that the same thing as making disciples? What does this look like for girls ministry?

I want to leave you with this excerpt from Charles Spurgeon to summarize the heart of what it looks like to disciple, and I hope it gives you a sweeter image of girls ministry through the lens of Acts 1:8.

Dear friends, we are to be witnesses of what Christ has done. If we have seen Christ, if we believe in Christ, let us tell it honestly. These apostles had a great deal to tell. They had been with Christ in private; they had seen his miracles; they had heard his choicest and more secret words; they had to go and bear witness to it all. And you, who have been let into the secrets of Christ, you who have communed with him more closely than others, you have much to tell. Tell it all, for whatever he has said to you in the closet you are to proclaim upon the housetop. You are to witness what you have seen, and tasted, and handled, concerning your Lord.

You are to witness to what he has revealed, to make known to others the doctrine that he preached, or taught by his apostles. Mind that you do not tell any other. You are not sent to be "an original thinker", to make up a gospel as you go along; you are a witness, that is all, a retailer of Christ's truth, and you miss the end of your life unless you perpetually witness, and witness, and witness to what you know of him, and to what you have learnt from him.[2]

EFFECTIVE DISCIPLESHIP IS OUR FULL RELIANCE ON THE HOLY SPIRIT AND COMPLETE SURRENDER TO THE TRUTH THAT JESUS IS WITH US ALWAYS, TO THE END OF THE AGE.

REACHING THE GIRL

I can't wait to move out.

I HATE MY BODY AND I'VE TRIED TO STARVE MYSELF MULTIPLE TIMES.

I text and drive.

IT'S NO ACCIDENT THAT YOU ARE AN INFLUENCE OVER HER. STEP INTO THE CALLING GOD HAS PLACED ON YOUR LIFE.

CHAPTER 3

IN YOUR CIRCLE

When you picked up this book, you were already thinking about a group of girls or maybe just one girl God has entrusted you with. Let me just stop right here and thank you. This likely shows how serious you take the calling God has placed on your life, and I want you to know that God will honor your faithfulness in how you are stewarding this responsibility.

I often get emails from people asking the best way to start a girls ministry. They feel like God has put a passion in their hearts to start a ministry or a non-profit organization that reaches teen girls. Every time I reply to one of these emails, I begin with a question: Who are the girls in your life, and where are you already ministering?

If I have said this once, I'll say it a million times before this book is over. Girls ministry isn't complicated. It's not a program you need to start or an organization that needs funding. Where does girls ministry start? How do you begin? With the girls right in front of you.

As we continue to wrestle with this concept, here are the two questions I want to challenge you with this chapter:

1. Who has God placed right in front of you?
2. How do they need you?

The way you answer these questions is going to be the driving force behind your how. There is no one-size-fits-all in girls ministry, so you are going to have to spend some time defining your personal girls ministry in order to be most effective where God has placed you.

Let's first talk about *who* the girls right in front of you are. Because I know there are student pastors, coaches, teachers, and moms and dads reading this, the girls in front of you will look different for everyone. To get you started answering that first question, look at the list below and consider who comes to mind:

- Your daughter(s)
- Your friends' daughters
- Your daughters' friends
- Your girls small group, Sunday school class, or Bible study
- Girls in student ministry
- Girls who serve alongside you at church
- Girls who you coach, lead, or teach

What girls came to mind when you read the list? What names surprised you? (Feel free to skip to the chart on page 44 if you want to go ahead and write their names down.)

If you're a parent, it's probably a given that your daughter would make the list. Or if you're a student pastor, the girls in your student ministry are an obvious answer. But look beyond the obvious and ask God to open your eyes to who else you have influence over as a minister of teen girls.

This is where girls ministry begins—with this list of girls right in front of you. These are the girls who the Lord has already entrusted you with. They're right here in front of you, and they need you.

But you may be thinking, *Why do they need me? Isn't someone else qualified for this? Doesn't she have a mom for that? Isn't that the job of the women's minister?*

We'll get more into how all of our roles work together in Part Two of this book, but you can't move forward unless you see the value you play in these girls' lives. In order to see your value, we must first look at the girls' needs both in the long run and today.

A LIFELONG IMPACT

Here's a statistic from Lifeway Research looking at the dropout rate of teens:

> While sixty-nine percent say they were attending at age seventeen, that fell to fifty-eight percent at age eighteen and forty percent at age nineteen. Once they reach their twenties, around one in three say they were attending church regularly.[3]

And friends, this research was done in 2019. Think of how those numbers have changed since. Check out another statistic from Lifeway Research about this same topic:

> Teens who had at least one adult from church make a significant time investment in their lives also were more likely to keep attending church. More of those who stayed in church—by a margin of 46 percent to 28 percent—said five or more adults at church had invested time with them personally and spiritually.[4]

That's an eighteen percent increase in the likeliness that teens will continue following Jesus after graduation if just five or more adults invest in and disciple them as teens.

Scott McConnell, who lead this research study, said this of meaningful relationships within the church:

> Investment time in young people lives out the love of Jesus Christ in a tangible way. It proves that a young person belongs at church.

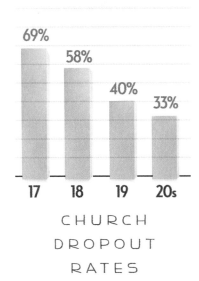

C H U R C H
D R O P O U T
R A T E S

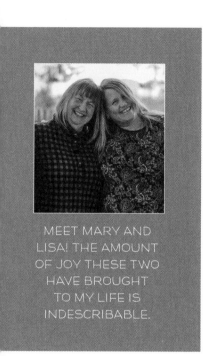

MEET MARY AND LISA! THE AMOUNT OF JOY THESE TWO HAVE BROUGHT TO MY LIFE IS INDESCRIBABLE.

CHECK OUT THE PODCAST HERE:

It can help connect the dots to help a teen integrate their faith into their life. And it gives the teen a connection to church after graduation when many of their peers are no longer around.

Anybody wondering if they can make a difference can stop wondering. One Sunday school teacher, one chaperone, one discussion leader, one person at church who clearly cares can impact the course of a teen's spiritual journey.[5]

The teen girls right in front of you need you. Like McConnell said, stop wondering if it's worth it! It's a proven fact that you can make a difference in their walk with Jesus. They may never write you a card or even say thank you to your face, but the time and energy and commitment you make to these girls matters today, and it matters twenty, forty, and sixty years from now.

When I think about my own life, I think about my Sunday school teachers from my middle and high school years. There were two women who spent every year and almost every Sunday with me: Mary Stevenson and Lisa Fox. They were the moms of my friends, but they were also some of the most dedicated Sunday school teachers and small group leaders I've ever known.

To this day, they are women I love and admire. I can almost guarantee that I never told them when I was in high school, but I know today how much of a role they played in my desire to live for Jesus after graduation. Their "momentary" discipleship during those years impacted my eternity, and I will never forget it.

SEEING THE NEEDS FOR TODAY

If you are familiar with Lifeway Women, you have probably heard of the Marked Podcast. Kelly King and Elizabeth Hyndman are fun and engaging hosts of helpful conversations. In early 2022, they reached out to me about an idea for a podcast called, "What I Wish My Parents Knew." (I know I have the interest of the parents reading this book, but the rest of you, keep reading. It's so good!)

I put together a survey and sent it to girls ministers all across the country to share with the girls in their ministry. Teen girls were able to fill out this survey anonymously, and the answers they provided were so helpful for this conversation.

The first survey question: If you could tell your parents anything (with no consequences), what would it be?

Check out some of their answers:

I TEXT AND DRIVE.

I MISS MY BIRTH PARENTS.

SOMETIMES, I DON'T WANT TO BE HERE.

THEY SHOULD'VE PAID ATTENTION TO US FROM THE BEGINNING.

MY STRUGGLE WITH MASTURBATION.

I FEEL LIKE YOU DO NOT SUPPORT WHAT I WANT TO DO (MISSIONS).

I LOVE THEM SO MUCH, NO MATTER WHAT I TELL THEM, OR WHAT I DO, OR WHAT THEY DO.

I CAN'T WAIT TO MOVE OUT.

HOW I'M STRUGGLING WITH SEXUAL SIN AND CAN'T FIND MY WAY AWAY FROM IT NO MATTER HOW HARD I PRAY OR TRY.

THEY NEED TO START FOCUSING ON GOD AND NOT THEMSELVES.

HOW MUCH I HATE MY BODY AND THAT I'VE TRIED TO STARVE MYSELF MULTIPLE TIMES.

I LIKE A GUY THAT MY PARENTS DON'T LIKE.

I'M NOT LIKE MY SISTERS, AND I HATE BEING COMPARED TO THEM.

I THOUGHT I LIKED GIRLS FOR A MOMENT.

LITERALLY EVERYTHING I'VE BEEN KEEPING FROM THEM.

Do you know the needs I see in this list?

- I see girls who need a safe place to talk about the hard stuff.
- I see girls who need people to speak truth over them in love.
- I see girls who need people to hold them accountable.
- I see girls who need to know how much they are loved.
- I see girls who need to know they can find freedom in Christ.
- I see girls who need to find their value in the way God sees them.

What other needs do you see in this list? Use the space below to write them down. Think about the girls right in front of you. Where do you see their hurts? Their misconceptions? Their hopes and desires?

These girls are right here in front of you with big needs. And I want you to note that these girls are in church or have Christian parents. It's easy to assume that the girls in church don't struggle with sin or doubt like those who aren't in a Christian home. But we can't ignore their needs or pass off the responsibility to someone else.

You might've read that list of things girls didn't believe they could share with their parents and thought, *Oh, that's not my child!* Or, *Sounds like these girls just need better parents!* But the reality is that this survey helped us to see that the majority trust and love their parents.

Here's the real impressive result we got from this survey. We asked, "If your parents know Jesus, do they live out what they preach?" On a scale of one to five (five being perfectly), seventy-one percent of girls answered either four or five. That's huge!

This shows that the issues teen girls are struggling with have to be seen and met beyond just their parents (even if they are godly and loving and present in their lives). Teen girls need their parents, student pastors, girls ministers, teachers, best friends, Sunday school teachers, and so many others to meet them where they are and to disciple them.

Don't ignore the girls right in front of you. It's no accident that you are in their lives. Step into the calling God has placed on your life, and trust His faithfulness in saving and leading girls into a lifelong journey with Him.

This is girls ministry.

STEP INTO THE CALLING GOD HAS PLACED ON YOUR LIFE, AND TRUST HIS FAITHFULNESS IN SAVING AND LEADING HER INTO A LIFELONG JOURNEY WITH HIM.

GO TO SCHOOL LUNCHES, SPEAK AT THEIR PRACTICES, BRING POPSICLES TO THEIR GAMES, ATTEND THEIR CONCERTS—JUST BE THERE AND BE CONSISTENT.

REACHING THE GIRL

CHAPTER 4

OUTSIDE YOUR CIRCLE

I've always found the easiest part of girls ministry to be reaching out to the girls right in front of me. Then, I don't have to put much effort into finding girls to build relationships with. But let's rewind to 2019 when they were no longer right there in front of me.

I served on staff at a church for nine years in the city where I had given my entire life to doing ministry. But with God's call to move to Nashville to begin my work at Lifeway, the ministry that I had spent years establishing was suddenly gone.

Of course, I would still FaceTime and text the girls I had been pouring into for years, but it was different. New leaders were stepping up in the church and loving them well, and I found myself in a new city with no church and no community.

I see now that God was using that transition as a healing and refining tool in my life. But it was a really strange place to be. I longed to have relationships and to disciple teen girls, but I didn't know where to begin. I was a mom with a four-month-old daughter trying to learn the ins-and-outs of my new career. I didn't even have a church in my new city, let alone church community!

Finding a church didn't come easy, as many of you probably know. For months and months, we just couldn't find the right fit in a city full of churches. My husband and I came with our own baggage, and we were weary. It felt way easier to stay home on Sundays than to continue forcing ourselves to show up at churches that we didn't fit into. My desire to find community, biblical teaching, and ways to pour into others started to dwindle. I just didn't want to keep trying anymore. But then, by God's grace, we finally found a church—a large church. It was pretty much the opposite of what we were looking for, but it was clear that God had guided us there.

If you've ever been to a large church, you know that plugging in is quite challenging. There's nothing worse than trying to make friends or find a small group or choose where to serve when you feel like a tiny soul in a large sea of people. I remember thinking, *they've got plenty of people here to serve. They definitely don't need me.* However, God kept urging me to serve in student ministry. My response to Him was, "God, I want to be resting, not serving. We've barely settled in here. I literally know no one." God didn't seem to mind me whining about this not being a good time. He wasn't going to let me wallow because He was calling me to go. So I finally surrendered and intentionally began looking for places to serve. Slowly but surely, God began bringing teen girls into my life to disciple.

Here's the deal. Not knowing any teen girls wasn't an excuse for me to skip out on discipleship. It wasn't an excuse for me to sit comfortably at home on Sundays or just show up for morning service. It wasn't going to give me a pass on girls ministry, and it's not going to give you a pass either. And I think you know that too.

You're reading this book because you believe God is asking you to minister to teen girls. But what I want you to see is that God isn't just asking you to do ministry with the girls right in front of you. He is asking you to get uncomfortable. To put your preferences and comforts aside.

He wants to take you out of your normal routine and invite you into an abundant life of following Him.

This might be the encouragement some of you need to actually start serving in your local church. To open your eyes and see the girls who need you. But since many of you are already doing that and doing it well, I want to remind you: *don't stop here.*

As someone who has worked on church staff and served as a small group leader, I know how easy it is to get so narrow-minded and focused on only the girls right there with you inside the walls of a church or ministry or home. But there are so many girls who don't know Jesus, don't have loving parents, don't know what it means to be part of a church body, or don't have anyone meeting them where they are.

Because if you and I aren't the ones going after those girls, who will?

Are there any girls who come to mind that you know are not being reached and are missing discipleship and connection? Maybe some of the ideas below will help prompt you:

- The local high school girls' basketball team (or any other sports)
- Teen girls in foster care
- Local non-profit organizations, such as YoungLives, Fellowship of Christian Athletes (FCA), and Young Life
- Teen girls in your neighborhood

Now, I want you to hold your place here and skip over to the chart on page 44. Take some time listing names, organizations, and groups of girls that you might be able to reach where you are and with the tools God has already given you.

RELATIONSHIP > CHURCH INVITE

Every single teen girl needs to be met right where she is with the love of Jesus and the hope of the gospel. For many years, we have bought the lie that if we just get girls inside the walls of the church, we will see revival amongst their generation. But as I sit across the table from

EVERY SINGLE TEEN GIRL NEEDS TO BE MET RIGHT WHERE SHE IS WITH THE LOVE OF JESUS AND THE HOPE OF THE GOSPEL.

girls who are "churched" yet far from Jesus, it reveals that sitting in a building isn't what will lead to salvation.

Do we want girls in church? Yes! But the goal isn't church attendance or helping modify their behavior. We want girls who are in love with Jesus and committed to following Him. And if those are the girls we want in our churches, and in our schools, and in our homes, we must do more than hand out church invite cards. We must build gospel-centered relationships with them.

My friend, Rachel Frazier, has been doing girls ministry for years and has been a contributor on the Lifeway Girls blog several times. I came across a blog she posted in January 2020 that I still think is so important for us to read.

Here's an excerpt from Rachel's post about relationship building:

READ THE
FULL BLOG
POST HERE:

> I don't know about you, but I'm personally more inclined to listen to people I actually have a relationship with. And you can't make an impact on people to the fullest if you're not trying to be invested in their lives. You're not going to be able to build relationships *at church* with girls who *don't come* to church, which means you have to go to where they are! And not only that, you have to be consistent and show up. Go to school lunches, speak at their practices, bring Popsicles to their games, attend their concerts—just be there and be consistent.
>
> . . .
>
> When you show people you care about their personal story, you're able to usher them to THE story of Jesus through continual prayer and conversation.[6]

Remember, these girls aren't projects for you to convert into a number for attendance records—they're people with needs, hurts, wants, and desires. Sometimes, the best thing you can do for someone is to simply love them as the church.

The goal of the relationships you build with teen girls will always be to lead them to salvation in Jesus Christ and a lifetime of following after Him. However, teen girls don't want to hear what you have to say unless they know that you love and care for them. This applies to girls both inside and outside the church. However, the girls that don't go to church or live in a Christian home probably have a pretty skewed view of who Jesus is. The culture they are surrounded by 24/7 (thanks, social media!) is constantly trying to teach them a false theology about God. And on top of receiving false information about Jesus and the church, these girls also deal with those who call themselves "Christians" but don't actually live according to the truth of God's Word.

Friend, when you choose to reach the teen girls who need you, you might be the first person to share the real love of Jesus Christ with them. Jesus doesn't love those girls because He can check an item off a list or add to His numbers of followers. He loves them despite the fact that they are sinners, so much so that He died for them. And if Jesus was willing to do that for them, how can we show them His love in a tangible way?

In the blog excerpt on the previous page, Rachel mentioned some ways that might seem minor or like a waste of time. I mean, how is handing out Popsicles an expression of Jesus's love for teen girls? Spoiler alert: it's not the Popsicle (or the donut!). It's the fact that you are willing to set aside your time and preferences to build a relationship with teen girls who *might* one day be ready to trust and listen.

Girls ministry is a get-in-the-trenches kind of discipleship. We must meet girls where they are, consistently meet their physical needs in order to express the tangible love of their Savior, and then boldly proclaim the truth of the gospel. From there, the Holy Spirit must do His work. But prayerfully, over time, you will see girls come to know Jesus, and you be able to lead them as they walk faithfully after Him surrounded by a loving church community.

This is girls ministry.

Instructions: It's time to create a clearer idea of the teens girls in your life who God is calling you to disciple. Let me encourage you to spend some time writing those girls' names down. If you don't know their names, just write down a description that best fits (e.g., Sunday school girls, soccer team, daughter's school friends, etc.).

GIRLS IN YOUR FAMILY

GIRLS IN YOUR CHURCH

GIRLS IN YOUR COMMUNITY

GIRLS IN YOUR NEIGHBORHOOD

PART 2

THE PEOPLE IT TAKES:
LINKING ARMS

It was just six days ago as I was getting ready for a long overdue breakfast with one of my discipleship girls when my world stopped. At 9:06 a.m., I received a text from a girls minister friend that felt like a punch right in the gut: "I just got the devastating news about Steph Williford passing away. Just can't believe it."

I think I read that text about twenty-five times before I could fully grasp what I was reading. How was it that my friend who I had just been texting a few days ago was now gone? What about all the plans we were making for girls ministry? How could God take someone at thirty-eight years old who was thriving in ministry? What about all of the people who loved her? What about her teen girls?

It is no mistake that I'm writing this chapter on the same day so many remember and grieve the life of an incredible minister. To know Steph was to love Steph. And to know Steph was to be loved by Steph. Here's a short summary from her obituary that beautifully described Steph's heart:

> Her whole heart belonged to the Girls' Ministry. It was her soul's calling to point everyone to Jesus at every big or small opportunity. Whether it was hosting epic events for thousands or attending high school football games just to see one of her girls do a three-minute dance number, Steph was intentional about the way she loved her people.
>
> Those who knew Steph would agree she was the epitome of JOY. She was everyone's cheerleader and always found a reason to turn any negative into a positive and any meeting into a party. On any given day, you could find Steph wearing glitter, tulle, or animal print, and she always had a spare set of supplies for every possible situation. The party didn't truly start until Steph arrived. Imagine the party she's experiencing today![7]

My heart lit up earlier this week when my phone rang with a call from Erin. She was a longtime friend of Steph's and worked in girls ministry alongside her for years. For the next half hour, we cried and remembered Steph through countless stories and memories. It was so good for my soul. Not just to remember Steph but to remember her ministry mattered. To remember our people matter.

And yes, Steph rocked the pink for teen girls and threw the best events. But we all loved her for the way she loved, served, and discipled others in the name of Jesus.

Friends, I want to be like Steph. I want a legacy of ministering to teen girls that is marked by the way I loved, served, and discipled others. And the beauty of that is I don't have to be a Steph—in fact, I can't be! And it's not because I don't own anything pink or glittery. It's because God didn't form me or fashion me to be a Steph. He made me to be Amanda with my own unique gifts, talents, and a closet full of neutrals.

God didn't make you to be a Steph either. (Guys, you're probably taking a deep breath of relief right about now.) But just because you aren't a Steph, doesn't mean you don't have a significant role to play in girls ministry. Whether you are a parent, a person on church staff, a volunteer, or a teen girl yourself, you are not just wanted for girls ministry, you are needed.

Just like 1 Corinthians 12 talks about the body of Christ needing different members, girls ministry falls in that same category. The truth is that the burden of one person's discipleship is too big for any of us to carry single-handedly. We are broken, sinful people who have weak spots that—listen to this—can't (hand clap) do (hand clap) it (hand clap) all (hand clap). The ear can't see for the eyes, and the eyes can't hear for the ears. The hands can't walk like the feet, and the feet can't feed our mouths like our hands can.

It should be a comfort to us to know that moms can't fulfill the roles of dads, and dads can't fulfill the roles of moms. Parents can't replace the importance of a student minister, but student ministers do not take away the importance of a parent's influence and discipleship. Oh, and teen girls? We desperately need them to love their younger sisters in the unique ways God has gifted them.

For far too long, we've placed the weight and pressure of discipling teen girls on the shoulders of one person. But we are all needed, and we all need each other. Because it's a team effort—a whole body of Christ effort—to effectively disciple teen girls.

IT'S A TEAM EFFORT—A WHOLE BODY OF CHRIST EFFORT—TO EFFECTIVELY DISCIPLE TEEN GIRLS.

WOMEN

DON'T MISS WHAT GOD HAS RIGHT IN FRONT OF YOU TODAY.

CHAPTER 5

IN MINISTRY

I've never been a "girls minister." Say whatttt?? I know! But it's true. When I began serving in this position with Lifeway Girls, I felt like such a fraud and extremely inadequate. How was I supposed to serve girls ministers if I had never been one? Would they ever respect me or welcome me in? I've never walked in their shoes or even thrown a girls only event.

But as the sweet community of girls ministers welcomed me with the most gracious and loving arms (Steph Williford being one of the first!), I realized how much I had in common with girls ministers. It was during these first few months of being thrown into the girls ministry world that my perception and understanding of girls ministry was forever changed. And I quickly realized that in my years of working on church staff, I was in fact a girls minister without the title.

Even though I started working for the church part-time at age fifteen, it wasn't until I was twenty-one and working full-time that I finally began working with student ministry. I wasn't on the student ministry team but served multiple ministries. My official title was Campus Ministry

Assistant. (Real life: I only received this "fancy" title because I asked for business cards, and our church didn't give business cards to admins. So I was really just an admin with business cards). Throughout my six and a half years in this role, I did everything from rapping the books of the Bible with our kids ministry on Wednesday nights to overseeing our hospitality ministry to taking care of the campus budget and serving our student pastor when everything else didn't consume me. And while the parking team of men all over the age of fifty will always have a special place in my heart, it was whenever I got to serve with the student ministry that my heart soared.

I never had the title of girls minister, and I never desired to be the girls minister (because teen guys are so stinking awesome, too!). But my position on the church staff granted me opportunities to minister to teen girls. Not only was there a need for a female staff person to counsel a teen girl (spiritually or emotionally) or lead the next Bible study, but I was always at the church. When a new teen girl walked in, I was the first face they often met. If the parents of a teen girl needed advice about a difficult situation, I was the one pulled into the conversation with the student pastor. And when I needed help setting up or tearing down for an event, there were plenty of teen girls to help. Eating at Chick-fil-A after church every single Wednesday night with the other staff members and their families meant that there were tables full of girls eating right beside us. So I was a campus ministry assistant with the honorary, coincidental position of girls minister.

Let me ask you. What is your position as a woman in ministry? Are you a women or kids minister? An admin or ministry assistant like I was? A volunteer student minister who is also the pastor's wife and has a full-time job on the side? Or maybe you are one of the few women who is called a girls minister?

No matter what your job title says, you are a girls minister, even if you have never been given the official role. And if you are the girls minister, I know that you do way more than just girls ministry. Regardless of titles, your position as a woman in ministry matters significantly in the lives of teen girls. And while that might feel exhausting, complicated, and out of reach most of the time, I want you to know and believe that teen girls need you, and you are extremely valuable in your role.

The more women I talk to in different ministry positions, the more I realize that we have many of the same struggles. But we also have many of the same opportunities and gifts. I hope my own experiences, my own struggles, and my own mistakes will encourage you in your discipleship journey.

I *loved* my time on church staff, but I faced many challenges. The church culture often made it challenging for me to grow and lead in my role. At first, I felt like I was given the freedom to participate and serve and offer ideas for things I was passionate about (a.k.a. student ministry). But the longer I was on staff, the more I was reminded of the limitations within my position and title. Being a ministry assistant felt like a restraint more than a gift. I struggled with feeling good enough to have a seat at the table, and I never felt like I had the space or support to be more of who God had called me to be.

There will be times and seasons when you are undervalued, overlooked, and even mistreated. I hate it, and I'm sorry if that's you. I know you bring so much to the table in your churches and ministry contexts. I wish I could look you in the eyes right now (and even go back to twenty-five-year-old me) and remind you that we don't need fancy titles to make an impact. You might not be doing what you want to be doing ten years from now, but I don't want you to miss what God has placed right in front of you today. Your title might not allow you to teach from a stage, or participate in certain meetings, or get a say in where the budget money goes, but you have a responsibility to steward the gifts and talents the Lord has given you right now.

That doesn't mean you throw your hands up and say, "Well, I guess I'm stuck here forever, so I don't need to work toward what God has called me to be." That's a lie.

NO MATTER WHAT YOUR JOB TITLE SAYS, YOU ARE A GIRLS MINISTER, EVEN IF YOU HAVE NEVER BEEN GIVEN THE OFFICIAL ROLE. AND IF YOU ARE THE GIRLS MINISTER, I KNOW THAT YOU DO WAY MORE THAN JUST GIRLS MINISTRY.

Some of you are in your dream role. But I have a feeling others might not want to serve in their current position for the next fifty years or even plan to be on ministry staff this time next year. Either way, through your faithfulness today, you are planting seeds that will grow and branch for years to come. This brings to mind Galatians 6:7-9:

> Don't be deceived: God is not mocked. For whatever a person sows he will also reap, because the one who sows to his flesh will reap destruction from the flesh, but the one who sows to the Spirit will reap eternal life from the Spirit. Let us not get tired of doing good, for we will reap at the proper time if we don't give up.

What is God asking you to sow in your current situation? Don't say, "That's not in my job description, so that's not my responsibility." Teen girls are watching you. Teen girls need you, even if you are a women's minister, preschool director, or are the world's greatest church admin. And teen girls are learning from you, even if you rarely interact with them or invite them into your inner circle.

But are you making an effort to minister to these girls? Are you making the most of the position God has put you in? Are you using your voice to speak on their behalf? Are you inviting them to serve alongside you? Do you see them with the same eyes and heart as your heavenly Father? Or are you more like me? Missing out on simple discipleship moments right in front of you.

Yes, you might be at a church that doesn't include "teen girl discipleship" in your job description. Or you might be in a place that discourages you from using your gifts as you thought you'd be able to use them. Or you might have a title or position that holds you back, but you don't have a God who holds back from you.

Let me repeat that: you do not have a God who holds back from you.

He might have you in a difficult season or a position that you don't love. You might not be able to understand how God wants to you use you to minister to teen girls quite yet. But He is a good Father who withholds

YOU DO NOT HAVE A GOD WHO HOLDS BACK FROM YOU.

no good thing (Ps. 84:11), and He knows what we need more than we ever could. And just like Esther, He has placed you in your position for "such a time as this" (Esth. 4:14), if only you will be obedient to His calling and His Word.

Trust Him in that. Trust Him with your position and title. Trust Him with your current season. And trust that He can use you to minister to teen girls right where you are and with what you already have. Because what God can do is "above and beyond all that we ask or think according to the power that works in us" (Eph. 3:20).

WE NEED MEN IN
MINISTRY WHO
ARE BOTH WILLING
AND PASSIONATE
ABOUT SEEING TEEN
GIRLS THRIVE IN A
RELATIONSHIP WITH
JESUS CHRIST.

MEN IN

CHAPTER 6

MINISTRY

Who would've ever thought that men would get their own chapter in a book about girls ministry? Well, here we are, and I'm seriously so grateful to have a girls minister like you to partner with as we disciple teen girls together.

At a recent student ministry event, I was hanging out at the Lifeway Girls booth handing out free coffee mugs to promote our upcoming event. Every female leader that walked up to the booth lit up with excitement reaching for a free mug. However, as you can expect, it was quite amusing to hand guys a coffee mug with "Girl" written on it. The reactions were all over the place. Some guys were surprised to even be acknowledged, some were thrilled and exclaimed, "I only have girls in my student ministry right now," and some chuckled and politely declined.

However, there were a few hard pushbacks from a couple of men. As graciously as I could, I'd ask them if they had girls in their ministry, and they'd say, "Yep." And I would smile and say, "Then did you know you're a girls minister?"

The shock and despair on these men's faces said it all. One guy put the mug down and declared, "I will *not* be called a girls minister," as he quickly walked off in disbelief.

Clearly, it was not my best marketing approach, but the statement is true. You might be a man in ministry, but if you've been entrusted with teen girls, then you are a girls minister. Whether you're a worship pastor, student intern, senior pastor, or (fill-in-the-blank) in ministry, you have a role in discipling teen girls.

So before we go any further, I just want to thank you for being one of the brave men to pick up a book with sprinkled donuts on the cover. Clearly, you are feeling the weight of having teen girls in your ministry, and I know that can be really intimidating and scary—especially for men in ministry! There have been so many accusations, mishaps, and downright scandals that we've had to put restrictions in place when it comes to how men inside the church connect with teen girls.

However, somewhere along the way many have intentionally, or unintentionally, created so much space between themselves and the teen girls in their ministry that they are no longer truly able to disciple them. And while I will never be the person to tell you to go get coffee one-on-one with a teen girl, I will say that you are uniquely gifted and called by God to minister and disciple teen girls.

Yes, there are incredible godly women who get to connect with teen girls in ways that you won't be able to. But it is not their responsibility to be the only soul caretakers for those girls. And if you're married, your wife might be amazing and incredibly gifted in girls ministry, but you don't get to pass off the burden for her to carry alone.

We need men in ministry who are both willing and passionate about seeing teen girls thrive in a relationship with Jesus Christ. We need you. And because I know most of you love a good three-point sermon followed by an invitation, I'm going to use that format to demonstrate what it looks like for you as a man in ministry to point teen girls to Christ.

YOU MIGHT BE A MAN IN MINISTRY, BUT IF YOU'VE BEEN ENTRUSTED WITH TEEN GIRLS, THEN YOU ARE A GIRLS MINISTER.

1 YOUR EXAMPLE

Growing up as a teen girl without a Christian dad, I was constantly watching to see what a man who truly follows Jesus looks like. And the only place I really spent any significant time around godly men was at church. This means that the greatest examples of what I was longing to see were men in ministry.

These men helped teen-girl-me answer questions like, "Can a guy actually be fun and love Jesus at the same time?" "Does loving Jesus make a guy love other people better?" "What does it look like for someone to practice what they preach?" "Can I trust men?"

These questions feel weighty, and it's because they are. However, the student pastors and worship pastors that came and went during my teen years were some of the most influential people in my life. I wanted to be around them, I wanted to learn from them, and I wanted to know men who loved Jesus authentically because I didn't know it anywhere else.

So, how do you become a godly example to teen girls?

First, be a servant in your ministry. Do you lean toward being a delegator of tasks, or are you willing to serve others whatever the task may be? Teen girls won't remember how great a pastor is at giving directions or how leaders respect his authority. They will remember the men who served their leaders and students in his ministry. The ones who showed up early to help set up and were there to clean up at the very end. The ones who picked up trash and waited until the last student was off the bus.

Recently, my church hosted a girls ministry event, and I got to watch the guys on our student ministry team help in a way that I've honestly never seen. They were there for hours helping set up, collect trash, move tables, serve lunch, perform lip-sync battles, and whatever else was needed of them. They probably have no idea what a significant example they set for those girls that weekend simply by being willing to leave their comfort zones in order to serve others.

Next, don't take yourself too seriously. Girls want to have fun, and they want to see how you will lead in that fun. My student pastors could crush a sermon on the Trinity or the holiness of God, but they were also wild and hilarious. I mean, we had an event called the "Weinerthon." I'm not sure how our church didn't get in trouble for that, but I never questioned if I'd have fun in student ministry. Because following Jesus isn't boring! And I loved that I could bring my non-Christian friends to church knowing that those men would naturally create an environment where people would want to be.

Finally, if this applies to you, show them what godly priorities look like when it comes to family. We'll talk more about connecting with students in the next section because that is essential to girls ministry. However, teen girls need to see men who prioritize and love their families more than their jobs, their friends, and their ministries. So many girls have extremely broken homes and have no idea what a healthy marriage or good dad looks like. This means that they need to see you love your wife well. So don't just tell everyone how hot your wife is, but actually show these girls how much you treasure and respect her. And if you're a dad, let them see what it looks like for you to show up for your kids, apologize for mistakes, and beam with pride because of who they are.

You can probably think of a hundred other ways your example impacts teen girls because everything you do is influential in some shape or form. So, how does your influence point to your relationship with Jesus? How does your example make girls want to know and love God more? What does your influence reveal about your character?

Before moving forward, take some time to reflect on how you would answer those questions. Are there any changes you need to make or things that you need to work on?

2 YOUR CONNECTION

This may be the scariest part for men in ministry. How do you connect with a teen girl when you've never been a girl? You don't know why she's crying. You aren't sure how to respond when she tells you the same story about her cat for the seventh time this month. You don't know what to do when she says she is struggling with body image and an eating disorder. And please, no one bring up the time of the month.

If you've been in ministry and around students for any amount of time, I can imagine you've had a lot of awkward moments when you didn't know how to relate to or connect with them at all. And I'm here to tell you, welcome to the club! We all feel that.

Teen girls can be really complicated and awkward and often uncomfortable to be around. But they don't have to know you think that. What they need to know is that you care about them and love them despite the weirdness and the inability to relate.

Do you know her name?

Do you know what her family is like?

What sports does she play?

Why does she hate sports?

Who is her small group leader?

How long has she been involved in your ministry?

Is she really following Jesus?

These questions take time to answer because connection doesn't happen overnight. When a girl stops to talk and interact with you, make an effort to make her feel seen and known. This is as simple as acknowledging her and what she is saying to you without being distracted or belittling how she feels. It can be difficult at times, but I promise it's not complicated. Just meet her where she is and love her like Jesus does.

3 YOUR MESSAGE

I was sitting in a circle of twenty-three teen girls earlier this week as they each took turns sharing where they are in life and what God is teaching them. One of those girls shared about how God was convicting her in the way she was treating her friends, and it was her student pastor's sermon that led her to realize what she was doing was wrong.

I'm going to assume you know this, but I'm saying it anyway. The messages you teach or preach matter deeply for these teen girls' spiritual walks.

When I think back to my own time in student ministry, I still remember learning theology and how to study the Bible on my own from my student pastors. They were so faithful in teaching Scripture, and it was significant to what made me want to go into ministry myself. However, do you know what disengaged me almost immediately? The 183rd sports analogy. And I like sports.

You are going to lean heavily on what you know and what you love to shape your messages. However, if you want to be a girls ministry champion, find godly women in your life to speak into how you teach girls. These women not only can help you think through examples that relate better to teen girls, but they are also going to be the best people to give you feedback about things like sermon topics and the tone of voice you use while preaching. (And those women you love and admire enough to give feedback and insight into your messages are most likely voices that your whole student ministry deserves to hear from.)

Friend, your messages are incredibly impactful. But your teachings and sermons will be so much more life-changing for your teen girls (and teen guys too!) if what precedes you standing on a platform is your example and connection to them.

4 YOUR INVITATION

In your role in ministry, you are a gatekeeper to a world of opportunity for your teen girls to step practically into what it looks like to be a Christian woman. Often, all it takes is an invitation to step up and be involved. How are your girls gifted? What are they interested in? How can their gifts and interests be leveraged for the kingdom and in your ministry? We talked earlier about the importance of getting to know the girls in your ministry, but after getting to know them and earning a place of influence in their lives, the next step is to put them in positions to grow their faith through service and leadership. When my team and I were meeting to map out this book, one of my student pastors told me this story, and I want you to hear it from him.

After spending the first few months getting to know the student ministry as the new middle school pastor, I realized that the guys were all but checked out. Every time we asked students to volunteer for things, we had loads of girls jumping at the opportunity to serve and lead. While it was exciting to have so many students eager to jump in, the fact that none of the boys were stepping up kept me awake at night. After a little prayer and conversation with the lead student pastor, we decided to begin pointing out young men with leadership potential and intentionally discipling them to try to raise the level of involvement from our guys.

Five years later, I was the lead student pastor and had been steadily discipling the young men in the ministry. One Wednesday night, I preached a message that was meant to challenge students to come up with some creative ideas to reach their communities. At the end of the message, I asked students to raise their hands if they felt God calling them to step into this challenge, and in a room of nearly three-hundred high school students, there were guys' hands raised everywhere! The problem was that now there weren't any girls' hands in the air. What should have felt like a great accomplishment actually felt like a terrible failure. I had focused so single-mindedly on getting the guys engaged that I had left the girls behind.

As you reflect on this, spend some time answering the following questions: How are you intentionally inviting girls to follow Jesus? How can you better support and encourage their God-given gifts to help them live on mission? Who can you partner with in your ministry and church to create those opportunities?

YOU ARE A GATEKEEPER TO A WORLD OF OPPORTUNITY FOR YOUR TEEN GIRLS TO STEP PRACTICALLY INTO WHAT IT LOOKS LIKE TO BE A CHRISTIAN WOMAN.

MOMS

WHO BETTER
TO SHARE THE
BURDEN OF
PARENTING THAN
OUR PERFECT
HEAVENLY
FATHER?
BECAUSE LET
ME TELL YOU
THIS TRUTH:
GOD LOVES YOUR
DAUGHTER EVEN
MORE THAN
YOU DO.

&
DADS

The early days of parenting are physically exhausting. What is sleep? Where is my toddler? Does everyone have snacks? Did I drink too much caffeine today? (This is where I'm at as I write this. Prayers appreciated from you seasoned parents!)

From there, parents enter the mentally exhausting phase. Are my kids reaching milestones on time? Where should they go to school? Are they in enough activities? When do I need to talk to them about sex? Do they even know how to write a full paragraph?

And then comes the emotional and spiritual exhaustion phase of parenting—the teen years. How did she grow up so fast? She thinks I hate her. I don't even know what just happened. Did I do everything I could? What if I'm too late?

Spend some time journaling about where you are in this season of parenting. Use this space to write down your worries and fears, as well as your hopes and dreams for your teen girls.

No matter what stage of life, we can all agree that parenting is hard. But I want us to pause here and take a look at what Jesus says about burdens in Matthew 11. Read the verses below and spend some time meditating on Jesus's words.

"Come to me, all of you who are weary and burdened, and I will give you rest. Take up my yoke and learn from me, because I am lowly and humble in heart, and you will find rest for your souls. For my yoke is easy and my burden is light" (Matt. 11:28-30).

Raise your hand if parenting leaves you weary and burdensome! Raise your hand if you're looking for that easy yoke and light burden!

As Jesus calls you to parent your teen girls, it's not going to be simple or carefree. Taking up our cross to follow Him is what He has called us to do, but the parenting burden isn't ours to carry alone. We don't do it alone or out of our own strength. We lean into the Lord, acknowledge our weaknesses, and humble ourselves before the only One who sees our hearts and knows our needs better than anyone. He doesn't just see us and leave us our own. He offers to share the burden and provide you rest and sufficiency found in Him alone.

And who better to share the burden of parenting than our perfect heavenly Father? Because let me tell you this truth that I want you to write on your forehead so you don't ever forget it: *God loves your daughter even more than you do.*

My prayer is that you find freedom in this truth. Because even though I know you are the absolute best mom or dad for your teen girl, you can never replace or even compare to the love of her heavenly Father. Therefore, as you navigate these years, make sure to seek and rely on Him like your life and your daughter's life depends on it.

TO MOM

I know my mom is going to read this at some point, so let me start off by saying, "Hi, KK! This is for you."

My parents separated when I was ten years old, and I spent my teen years with a front row seat watching my mom raise me and my three siblings on her own. She'll be the first to admit that she was far from a perfect parent. However, there are some key truths that I love about my mom:

1. My mom wanted to protect her kids from experiencing pain and sorrow.
2. My mom wanted her kids to know and treasure God's Word.
3. My mom wanted to be a leading example of loyalty for her kids.

THIS IS MY MOM AND MY SISTER, SANDY! YOU CAN THANK MY MOM BOTH FOR FINDING THE PICTURE BELOW AND FOR THAT HAIRCUT.

The fourth truth would probably be that she gave me my love for sweets and donuts, but I figured the first three were probably the most important.

I love these things about my mom and her character hasn't changed in all these years. But these truths are extremely difficult when you are trying to be a mom to teen girls, and my mom can testify to this because she had three of us to deal with!

For starters, there was no way my mom could protect us from all the pain and sorrow this world and our choices would bring. She would've kept us in a plastic bubble for the rest of our lives if she could have, but we all had to take our own paths, figure out life, and make our own decisions. And there were often many, many, many consequences (sorry, Mom!).

By the time I could barely walk, I was signed up for Awana—a program for youth that emphasized Scripture memory. Any of you folks remember getting your Sparks vest? My mom wanted us in church, and she wanted us to know the Bible. I will never forget her trying to make up Bible verse songs to help me and wishing I was dead. I memorized more Scripture before I turned fourteen than I ever have as an adult, but do you think fourteen-year-old me ever thanked her or thought it mattered?

My mom is truly one of the most loyal people I've ever met—loyal to her family, her friends, her job, and her church. And while I often try to push her toward change, she is someone you can count on even if she doesn't agree with you (or even like you). I say this with firsthand experience because I have broken her trust, annoyed her beyond compare, and moved her grandbabies ten hours way, yet I know I can call my mom for just about anything at any time. That kind of relationship didn't start when I was already grown. It was something I knew as a teen.

So you sweet and precious moms reading this right now, here's what I want you to walk away with:

1. You can't protect her from everything.

I know, I know, *I know*. It's just plain awful. I only have a four-year-old daughter right now, and I already dread the teen years because of this. Your daughter will discover how broken this world is, she will mess up big time, and she will think you're wrong (ninety-nine percent of the time). However, it's not your job to have complete control over her. It's your job to show her the path and set the example, then put into the play the following two truths.

2. She won't realize the impact of knowing God's Word now, but she might one day.

I don't recommend singing Bible verse songs to her, but I do think she needs to know God's Word is number one. The biggest way you can do that is by making it a priority in your life. Go to church, get in God's Word on your own, and live out the truths you learn.

3. When everything falls apart, will she know she has you?

Your daughter can probably name the friends you don't like and the clothes you hate. She probably knows your biggest fear and your greatest weakness. But does she know that you are there? No matter what happens, or what mistake she makes, or whether or not she ever chooses to follow Jesus, does she know she has you and that your love for her will not sway?

This is a great time for you to put your book down and spend some time in prayer. Go to the Lord and ask Him to sanctify you. Make less of yourself and more of Him as you continue to be the mom you were made to be. Then, end in praise to God as you cling to our one main truth: *He loves your daughter even more than you do.*

TO DAD

Literally, it's 10 p.m. and I wanted to start my section to dads off with a solid dad joke. I texted my dad, and he came through for me right when I needed it the most!

My dad and I have a history of bittersweet memories. But getting to text him about jokes just now was the highlight of my day. Our relationship has changed over the years, but I'm so grateful for how it has grown.

I don't know what your relationship looks like with your daughter in this season, but can I just take a minute to say that you are the unspoken hero of girls ministry? The way she looks up to you, respects you, confides in you, and even argues with you shapes who she is becoming. How you live in light of being a dad matters significantly to your daughter's life now and eternally.

My husband, Brandon, was a natural dad from the time our kids took their first breaths. While I was trying to figure out which way was up, my husband was already the professional swaddler, changer, and soother in our family. He made it look easy and still does with the way he loves our kids so well.

Don't you wish you could make parenting a teen girl look easy? Well, while it may not be easy, it is worth it, and God has fully equipped you to be the best dad to your daughter. But it's probably not in the way you think.

Brandon is an incredible guitar player (and he also has the hair to go with it.) This past Christmas, he had an epic guitar solo to "Carol of the Bells." Did I mention his hair? It was perfect for it. And he literally crushed his solo. I've never fangirled so hard in my life. My four-year-old daughter on the other hand held her hands over both ears the whole time, then asked if we could leave mid-solo. She was unimpressed.

Even though her dad is the actual love of her life, she could not care less what he was doing on the guitar. However, the moment he came home that night, she ran and jumped in his arms like she does every single day. What's the difference? She cares so much about his being rather than his doing.

The same truth applies to your teen daughter just as it does my four year old. Your presence matters far more than your performance. It doesn't matter what day job you have, or what you can cook up in the kitchen, or what toilet you've successfully repaired that week. How do you show up for your daughter when no one is looking? How does she know that you are her safe place? What does she know and cherish about you? When do you spend time with her just because?

The other day I asked my daughter what she wanted to be when she grew up. She thought about it for a moment and answered, "I think I'll be brave and drive a Jeep like daddy." My husband drives a Jeep, that's it. We don't talk to her about Jeeps, and she rides in my minivan way more than she ever does in his truck. (Yes, he is the cooler parent. I know.) But how does she know he drives a Jeep? From being around him and spending time with him. Why does she want drive a Jeep like him? From being around him and spending time with him.

Your time and presence with your daughter are the two things she desires more than anything. There is no question that she will be influenced by you—the good, the bad, and apparently the car you drive. Therefore, be intentional with these teen years. You will have countless opportunities to be a significant influence of Jesus in her life. And while you are going to do that both in public and at home, the time you spend with her one-on-one will have the greatest impact.

YOUR PRESENCE MATTERS FAR MORE THAN YOUR PERFORMANCE.

I know you feel the weight of being a father right now. I don't think you'd be reading this if you didn't recognize the role you have in raising and discipling your teen girl. And while your daughter may never know you read this, I guarantee she will feel it without you ever speaking a word.

As you close this chapter, I want to give you the same prompt I gave the moms. Put your book down and spend some time in prayer. Go to the Lord and ask Him to sanctify you. Make less of yourself and more of Him as you continue to be the dad you were made to be. Then, end in praise to God as you cling to our one main truth: *He loves your daughter even more than you do.*

HE LOVES YOUR DAUGHTER EVEN MORE THAN YOU DO.

ONE FINAL THOUGHT: DON'T FORGET THE OTHER DAUGHTERS WHO NEED YOU TOO

If you asked me at any point who the most significant people in my relationship with Jesus were as a teen, it was my friends' parents. The Stevensons, the Foxes, the Overbeys, and so many more. They were the ones who stepped in when my parents couldn't, and they were the ones who showed me love and Jesus even though they had no obligation to do so.

Your daughter's friends need you. Whether their parents aren't in the picture or serve at church each week, they desperately need other godly parents to love them and teach them and show up for them. I can't encourage you enough to ask God to open your eyes to what that might look like.

Here are some significant moments I remember:
- The moms who drove me places and stayed up late talking.
- The dad who met my first boyfriend and showed me how to change my oil.
- The parents who took me in with no questions asked and treated me like their own.
- The mom who would make me call to say I got home safely.

- The dad who celebrated with me when I got my first job.
- The mom who let me cry when I was lonely.
- The parents who supported my mom as she navigated single parenting.
- The dad who showed me how to make a budget.
- The parents who paid for my lunch when we went out.

As parents, you want to pick and choose who your daughter becomes friends with. However, her friends (whether annoying or messy or broken or whatever) may be the exact girls that you are supposed to point to Jesus. All of these simple moments shaped my entire life, so I plead with you not to overlook the significance of the girls ministry available to you right there within the circle of your daughter's friends.

LOVING AND
LEADING MY GIRLS
MIGHT LOOK LIKE
USING FIFTEEN
MINUTES TO DROP
OFF COFFEE TO
A GIRL WHO IS
HAVING A DIFFICULT
WEEK OR SPENDING
TWENTY MINUTES
AFTER MY KIDS GO
TO BED CHECKING IN
WITH MY GROUP OF
GIRLS OVER TEXT.

CHAPTER 8

VOLUNTEERS

If you want to know what I loved most (and miss most) about my time on church staff, it was the volunteers who served alongside me. The ones who kept showing up week after week to be ministers of the gospel. The ones who came early and stayed late. The ones who held doors, washed dishes, stacked chairs, and fed many. The ones who prayed even harder than they worked. The ones who literally served the least of these and never complained one time. No one was paying them to be there and no one forced them to show up. So as a volunteer—either at a church or any other organization or ministry—please know that not only do you have such a special place in my heart, but you also serve a vital role in the body of Christ.

Before I ever worked at a church or became a mom or started my job at Lifeway, I was a volunteer. It is how I began my girls ministry and how I believe the most impactful ministry can be done. I have held the mighty and unpaid title of small group leader, discipleship group mentor, check-in and welcome host, D-Now and retreat leader, camp leader, mission trip volunteer, basketball coach, and probably ten others that I can't even remember. These roles were some of my favorites and I could spend hours telling you of the mundane moments that turned into life-changing discipleship through my time as a volunteer.

However, I want to get real with you. I struggle being a volunteer. And not in the I-think-I-should-be-on-church-staff way. I struggle because I often don't want to do it. I am the person thinking, *What excuse can I make so I don't have to show up for this?* It's easy to talk about how rewarding and life-giving and fun girls ministry can be, but we don't talk about the hard stuff. Volunteering is a constant giving up of your time, preferences, excuses, and life for free and for little appreciation. (I bet that isn't the sermon your pastor preached when he was trying to get you to sign up to serve.)

I talked about excuses in Chapter Three, and I want to share with you my four biggest when it comes to teen girl discipleship. These excuses are how I often want to justify why I can't serve, but they are real-life weaknesses in my life that I've had to learn to navigate as a volunteer. The more I recognize my weaknesses before an almighty God, the more I am able to experience His sufficient grace and power in me that Paul references in 2 Corinthians 12. Therefore, like Paul, "I will most gladly boast all the more about my weaknesses, so that Christ's power may reside in me. So I take pleasure in weaknesses, insults, hardships, persecutions, and in difficulties, for the sake of Christ. For when I am weak, then I am strong" (2 Cor. 12:9-10).

1 I DON'T HAVE TIME.

I'm a mom of two young children who works full-time, lives far from any family who can help, and has a husband who is busy running his own business. Most days, I literally don't have time to take a shower. From the moment I wake up until the time I close my eyes, I am constantly moving and doing to take care of my family. I feel like I have no time for anything extra in my life, especially when it comes to service and volunteer opportunities. I'm at my capacity, folks!

This is real life. I'm not lying when I say these things, so how on earth do I find time to meet with girls at Chick-fil-A once a week to talk about theology? The assumption I and many ministry volunteers make is that we need programmed times to do efficient ministry, such as saying, "If I can't give the same two hours every single week, there's no way that God can use me." But how silly is that? God doesn't work only in a Sunday school classroom or at your weekly Wednesday night service. He wants to use every moment, even your spare minutes, to bring the gospel to those around you.

I want to go to every student camp and be the leader that never misses a Sunday, but that isn't reality—especially in my current season of life. So instead of beating myself up for missing *another* small group gathering because my preschooler came home with *another* stomach bug, I remember God's grace and how He is the author of time. Therefore, I trust that He can use me to love and lead my girls in other ways that week. That could be using fifteen minutes to drop off coffee to a girl who is having a difficult week or spending twenty minutes after my kids go to bed checking in with my group of girls over text.

Volunteering in girls ministry is about showing up when you can and letting the girls around you know that you are a presence in their lives that they can count on. Your time will look different in every season of life, but that truth doesn't have to change. God doesn't care about your volunteer hours. He wants your heart.

Therefore, instead of worrying about the time you will be giving up, focus on how you can surrender your heart to Him. I promise that no matter what time you have to offer, He will always use a surrendered heart.

2 I DON'T HAVE THE "COOL FACTOR."

When I was in college, I felt cool enough to hang out with teen girls. But now I'm officially in my thirties, and my lack of relevance to teen girls has become an ever-increasing reality. I often joke that I'm always at least a year or two behind any trend. A few people around me will say, "Oh, that's not true. You are definitely cool." But that's just because they love me. The reality is:

GOD DOESN'T CARE ABOUT YOUR VOLUNTEER HOURS. HE WANTS YOUR HEART.

- White Nikes are officially outdated, yet I still wear mine daily.
- When I downloaded the BeReal app, my brother, who was twenty at the time, rolled his eyes and goes, "Yeah, that's for Millennials."
- I can't even count the number of times I've said, "Come watch this TikTok video!" instead of just saying, "Come watch this TikTok!"
- I drive a 2010 Honda Odyssey, and I am proud to say I fell asleep before 10 p.m. last night.

Anyone else feel old? If so, you're in good company! I've had countless conversations with people of all ages about not having anything to offer teen girls. We tell ourselves that girls need someone closer in age. One of the biggest lies I hear men and women tell themselves is, "My kids are old, and I'm not in that stage of life anymore. I've served my time."

Do you know where God mentions that age and a lack of coolness disqualify us from being disciple-makers? You already know you won't find it. In fact, He wants to use our irrelevance and our old-age wisdom to demonstrate to teen girls how to follow after Jesus for the long run.

Here's some good news. Teen girls don't want leaders or volunteers who act just like their friends. They want honesty and transparency and real-life people discipling them. They want and need you to be you. So, bring your un-coolness and join the club. I promise you'll be in good company and that God will use you exactly as He designed you to be.

BRING YOUR UN-COOLNESS AND JOIN THE CLUB. I PROMISE YOU'LL BE IN GOOD COMPANY AND THAT GOD WILL USE YOU EXACTLY AS HE DESIGNED YOU TO BE.

3 I DON'T HAVE IT TOGETHER.

Let me tell you a funny story. A few months ago, I was with my discipleship group at Chick-fil-A for our weekly meetup. Per the usual, I had my two young kids with me. Chick-fil-A is a great spot to meet because I can bring my four-year-old, and she can entertain herself on the indoor playground while I talk about God as a heavenly Father over some waffle fries.

This day, however, my child was in a whole mood that I was not prepared for. I had just finished talking about the story of the prodigal son, and how it demonstrates that God is the perfect Father. I even joked with my girls about how grateful I am that God is a perfect parent because I am far from it.

Not five minutes later, my daughter comes running out of the playground, and I invite her to sit with me and the girls for a minute. She yells, "*No!*" Then, she walks up to me and spits in my face in front of my group of teen girls. The girls gasped and watched in anticipation of what I would do next.

The timing of the whole situation made me question whether or not I should laugh or lose my mind. After I took a moment to breathe and respond with some kind of love, I had to discipline my daughter in front of my girls right there at Chick-fil-A.

I was honestly embarrassed and so frustrated that my girls had to see that. I texted them later to apologize, and they were incredibly kind. One of the girls responded and said, "We all babysit, so we understand. We're just so grateful you'll spend time with us." (Insert crying emoji)

My life is a mess. I am often late meeting with my girls, I have not prepared for many lessons, and I have gone to small group after fighting with my husband more than once. I am far from perfect. I feel like I often bring my leftovers to my teen girls. But God.

First Corinthians 2:1-5 says,

> When I came to you, brothers and sisters, announcing the mystery of God to you, I did not come with brilliance of speech or wisdom. I decided to know nothing among you except Jesus Christ and him crucified. I came to you in weakness, in fear, and in much trembling. My speech and my preaching were not with persuasive words of wisdom but with a demonstration of the Spirit's power, so that your faith might not be based on human wisdom but on God's power.

At the end of day, our testimony of girls ministry should never be, "Look what I did!" "Look how awesome I am!" "I'm so put together and knew all the right things to say!" No, girls ministry is all about, "Look what God did in spite of who I am." "Look at how awesome God is!" "I had nothing to offer, but God's Spirit did the work!"

It's okay if, like me, your life is a bit of a hot mess express. Because this is where we get to watch God demonstrate His power and kindness toward us despite our weaknesses, our messes, and our excuses.

HANNAH'S STORY

HANNAH AND I MET AT CAMP IN 2013.

Hannah is one of those girls who is full of life, but she has also walked one of the hardest roads. Hannah has battled depression and anxiety for as long as I've known her, and I've seen her at some of her darkest and lowest points.

I was in college when I first met Hannah. She was a high school student, and I adored her and her circle of friends. They were a ton of fun to be around, and they loved Jesus. But Hannah really wrestled internally with things, and I began meeting her one-on-one to see if I could figure out how to help. I'd pick her up, and we'd go get ice cream and walk the boardwalk at Yorktown Beach. She was always so quiet on those days—barely speaking more than a dozen words to me the whole time we were together. I'd ask questions and speak truth and Bible verses over her, but most of the time, we sat in silence. I was just there in the moment with her as I quietly prayed that she'd open up and that God would break down the barriers in her heart.

I did everything I could to help Hannah, but I never really saw the fruit of my time with her. She'd occasionally text me truths from God's Word that she was learning, or she'd open up about some of her struggles, but it often fell back into a cycle that I could never pull her out of.

Hannah would go off to college and face even more battles with depression and attempts at suicide. It was heartbreaking to watch from afar and feel completely helpless. At some point years later, God intervened and Hannah surrendered her life to Jesus! I remember crying at the photos of her baptism. I experienced firsthand how God is the only One who can save—not my time with her, not a Bible study, not anything I had to offer. Only God, and it was amazing.

THIS WAS AFTER A WEEKEND OF TOUGH CONVERSATIONS, BUT I SAW HANNAH GROW SO MUCH IN A FEW DAYS.

Fast-forward years later, Hannah is in medical school and on her way to becoming a doctor. Her life is an actual miracle. And while I was writing this book and thinking about her a lot, she texted me one random Thursday, and I have still not recovered from what she said.

Here are her words:

Hope you are doing well! I know this out of the blue, but it's been on my mind a lot recently, and I just wanted to say thank you for being there for me in one of the darkest times. For fighting with me, taking me to Chick-fil-A, spending time with me, praying with me. Words can truly never express how thankful I am to have had the love and support from people like you that were there for me. . . . Anyway, thanks for playing a role in making me who I am today—alive and thriving.

So to the volunteers spinning their heads trying to figure out how to help, remember this truth: You may never see the fruit of your work. You may not be the one who watches her surrender her life to Jesus or be there for her biggest life transitions. You may never hear from her again or know the impact you had.

While God doesn't work in your timing or in the way you think, He is always at work, and He is not wasting a single moment. The investment and time and prayers and care were monumental in Hannah's life.

She told me so herself:

Those days where we would walk in silence, or sit at Chick-fil-A, or drive down that one pretty road to Yorktown Beach, or walk through random stores are some of the times when I truly felt the most loved, cared for, and safe. I don't think I had the words to verbalize what I was going through internally, but you patiently continuing to support me through that was just enough to keep me going. If I knew we were meeting in two weeks, I had that hope to get me through two more weeks.

HANNAH MEETING BLAKELY FOR THE FIRST TIME IN 2018.

I think those are the moments that kept me alive. That gave me hope that maybe there is some God out there that truly loves me unconditionally, maybe there is more to life.

Keep showing up, keep leaning in, keep fighting for her. As a beloved daughter of God, she is worth it, and God will do what only He can do.

TEEN GIRLS ARE
THE EXPERT OF
TEEN GIRLS.

TEEN

CHAPTER 9

GIRLS

I've had the opportunity to teach at a few leadership training events through Lifeway Women called You Lead. These events happen all over the country, and I love getting to encourage and equip women to do girls ministry. It's very rare that I have more than a few dozen women in my breakout room, but the ones who are there want to be there. At three different events, however, there have also been teen girls in the room learning how to disciple and minister to teen girls. I'm not sure if they were there by choice or force, but each time I felt a different weight when I began to speak.

As I'm teaching and seeing the faces of those who are the goal of girls ministry, I'm reminded with every word that comes out of my mouth how much all of this actually matters. My stories and teaching didn't change just because there were teen girls in the room, but I quickly realized that I was not the expert. In each of those rooms, I said, "Do you want to know how to do girls ministry? Ask her," as I pointed to the girl sitting there intently listening. Teen girls are the expert of teen girls. No one is around teen girls more than other teen girls. We need to be talking less and listening to them more.

I might be a mom, or minister, or girls ministry specialist, but I am not a teen girl in today's world. I was one over a decade ago, but I have no clue what teen girls are facing or experiencing now in their day-to-day lives. While God doesn't waste my thirty-something-year-oldness, I can't offer what a teen girl has to offer to another teen girl. Things like friendship, real-life accountability, camaraderie, compassion, empathy, laughter, and admiration.

Those traits can be found among any of the other people listed in this book, but there's something so important to be found in a sisterhood between two teen girls. You are such a valuable piece of your friend, your sister, your youth group girls, or your teammate's journey with Jesus. Discipleship or mentorship isn't just reserved for those older or with more spiritual knowledge or experience. The only thing you need to start a girls ministry with the girls around you is a love for Jesus and a desire to see others know Him greater. You can do that right now, right here, exactly where God has placed you as middle or high school student.

But what does that actually look like? Let's talk about it.

Back in Part One, we addressed the two types of girls ministry: the girls right in front of you and the girls who need you. Just for a fun refresher, answer the following questions. (I've re-worded them a little for you this time.)

Who are the teen girls that you interact with on a regular basis?

Who are the girls you know but don't have any kind of friendship with?

_____

_____

_____

_____

_____

Isn't it so cool that God placed you uniquely where you are to build relationships with other girls in order for you both to know Him more fully? It's no accident that you're at your school (or homeschool), or on a that team, or in a specific club, or even at your church. God has wired you with certain desires and talents to connect with others. He wants you to see the good that can come from living with open eyes as you walk through your boring, routine days. (Hint: nothing is boring or routine to God.)

I want you to sketch out a "normal" day in your life on the following page. Add in times or descriptions or pictures—anything that helps you see what an average day looks like.

GOD HAS WIRED YOU WITH DESIRES AND TALENTS TO CONNECT WITH OTHERS. HE WANTS YOU TO SEE THE GOOD THAT CAN COME FROM LIVING WITH OPEN EYES AS YOU WALK THROUGH YOUR BORING, ROUTINE DAYS.

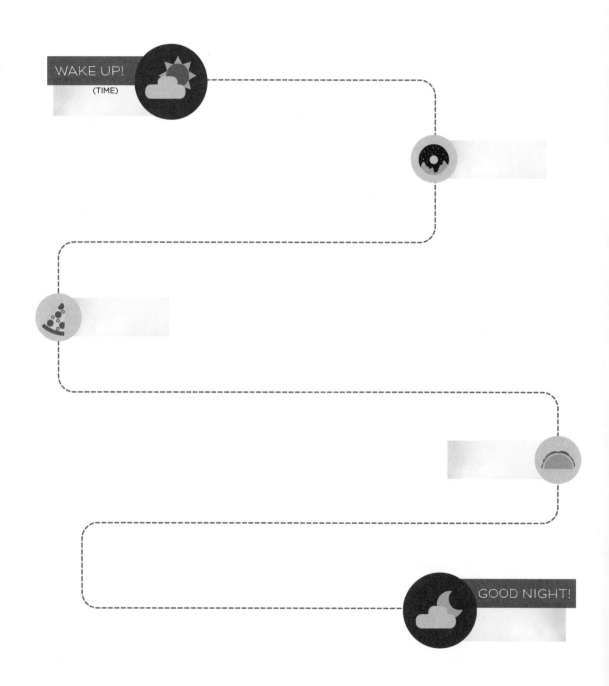

WAKE UP!
(TIME)

GOOD NIGHT!

86

Looking at this day, I want you to circle times when you could be more intentional for the kingdom of God. Maybe a time when you could be encouraging a friend who is hurt, or a part of your day when studying the Bible or praying with others could come naturally. Or maybe you see there are things in your day that are hindering your ability to follow Jesus.

This is not some feel-bad-that-every-second-of-my-day-isn't-sharing-the-gospel-with-someone activity. That's not the goal. However, I think it's so easy to forget how simple following Jesus in our daily lives can be. You might be the girl who starts a Bible study before school each week, or you could be the girl who spends the last fifteen minutes of her day praying for the lost friends in her neighborhood. You could be the teen girl who rallies other girls to start serving at a local soup kitchen, or God might be asking you to love your teammates more intentionally (since you're with them more than twenty hours a week!).

Don't believe the lie that you have to go on a foreign mission trip or be the weird church kid to make an impact for the kingdom of God. Will following Jesus make you do big things and look different from the rest of your friends—even your "Christian" friends? Absolutely. But all you have to do is faithfully follow Jesus in your daily walk and invite in the girls He has placed around you.

God doesn't want you to stay numb until college or leave the following Jesus stuff for when you're suddenly mature. I can imagine it's pretty intimidating to put yourself out there as a teen girl, especially one who proclaims to follow Jesus in a world that hates what He's about. But as you close this chapter today, please know that there will be countless other girls reading this with you. They are on mission to reach their friends, their school, and their teammates for Jesus, so you will never be alone, even if the journey feels isolating at times. And if no one else has verified your calling, let me be the first to say: *You are needed for the kingdom of God.* And if no one else has cheered you on, let me be the first to tell you: *I am pumped and so stinking proud of you.*

YOU ARE NEEDED FOR THE KINGDOM OF GOD. AND IF NO ONE ELSE HAS CHEERED YOU ON, LET ME BE THE FIRST TO TELL YOU: I AM PUMPED AND SO STINKING PROUD OF YOU.

MATCHING STORY

YOUR STORY HAS
SIGNIFICANT INFLUENCE.

CHAPTER 10

TO STORY

Writing this book has felt like an overflowing of my heart. It's my story written on these pages in order to connect with you and your story. It's probably the hardest part of this whole process because I'm being so vulnerable with you in sharing my life and the journey the Lord has taken me on. However, it is my story—not my degrees and not my job title—that has given me the ability to connect with you. And more than giving you a platform or a role, God has written your story to connect with teen girls and their stories.

So, what is your story? What's the journey God has taken you on? You're going to have a fun writing prompt on the following pages to help you sort this out a little bit. But I want to give you a little guidance before you begin.

First, be real. It's okay if you grew up in church, and it's okay if you just met Jesus last month! This is not the place to curate a fancy testimony of what God has done, but it's a chance to be real about what you've seen God do in and through your life. There's no set timeline for how it's supposed to happen or how it should look. Just remember that it has to be deeper than the highlight reel of your life.

Our most intentional friendships aren't just the people we share the good stuff with, right? They're the friends who know the good, the bad, and the ugly ugly. I'm not saying you need to air your dirty laundry out for everyone to see, but you also can't just talk about the joyful days of following Jesus and the victories from our sin. Make sure your story includes the real stuff, even if it's some of the hard stuff. Vulnerability is going to be your key to connecting with these girls.

Next, think of the girls in your life as you write. When we think about our stories in light of those we are trying to reach, God is often very gracious about bringing to light things we didn't even know mattered in our story.

Did you grow up without parents? Did you struggle with body image? How were you friendships? What decisions impacted you? How did Jesus change your life? Did that happen overnight or was it a process? What are you still learning? The way you answer these questions is how you will match story to story.

Finally, as you're writing, you might remember the stories of certain girls who don't necessarily relate to your story. It doesn't mean that your story doesn't matter, but it reveals the need for more than just your story. Your story has significant influence, but it can't be the only influence. Prayerfully consider people who might have stories that need to be invited into this girls ministry journey alongside you.

Write out your story on the following pages, including the low moments and the high. Make sure to add how you've seen God working in your life over the years. Highlight or underline the points of your story that God might be able to use in the discipleship of teen girls.

Who else do you need to invite to share their story with teen girls? How can you be the one to connect them?

PART 3

THE PLAN IT NEEDS:

RELATIONSHIP OVER EVERYTHING

Like just about anything in life, you aren't going to stumble into girls ministry. Even if your job title says girls minister or you have teen girls in your home, it still requires intentionality on your part to disciple teen girls effectively.

I know a lot of dads, moms, Sunday school teachers, mentors of teen girls, and student pastors. But I can only name about a dozen people who are intentionally seeking out ways to love and lead the teen girls in their lives. What makes them come across so intentional? It's their relational availability.

You can't look up relational availability in a Merriam-Webster dictionary, but think about the people in your life. Who is relationally available to you? Maybe it's your spouse who takes the time to ask how you're doing after a long week? Do you have an amazing group of friends who bring meals and gift cards after you've had an extensive surgery? What about that professor in college who spent time helping you master a difficult subject?

I challenge you to pause and really reflect on those people in your life who have shown up when no one else even knew you needed it. The people we surround ourselves with who are consistently concerned with us, even when it's inconvenient or unnecessary, are the people who leave lasting impressions on our lives. I challenge you right now to take a minute to text or pray for them before you keep reading.

Now that you've reflected on those incredible individuals in your life, I want you to think about the HOW and the WHY. Starting with the HOW, consider the following questions:

HOW did they show you love? _____

_____

_____

HOW did they make you feel seen?

HOW did they express care when you needed it?

HOW did they overwhelm you with encouragement?

HOW did they inspire you to follow after Jesus?

HOW did they speak truth in your life?

Now, let's address the WHY.

WHY did you need them?

WHY did you listen to or even believe them?

I CAN ONLY NAME ABOUT A DOZEN PEOPLE WHO ARE INTENTIONALLY SEEKING OUT WAYS TO LOVE AND LEAD THE TEEN GIRLS IN THEIR LIVES. WHAT MAKES THEM COME ACROSS SO INTENTIONAL? IT'S THEIR RELATIONAL AVAILABILITY.

WHY did you know they loved you? _____

_____

_____

WHY did they show up even when they didn't have to? _____

_____

_____

WHY did they make you want to know Jesus more? _____

_____

_____

The reason I want you to break down the how and why of the influential people in your life is because this is how you learn to be relationally available to the teen girls God has placed right in front of you. More than likely, your answers reveal that the people who invested in you and changed you weren't flippant about it. They didn't half-heartedly show care for you, or offer insincere encouragement, or only show up when it was convenient for them.

So, what are you doing for teen girls that someone else has already done for you? How are you making yourself available to them in a relational and intentional way?

I am sure there are people who showed up in big and extravagant ways in your life, and while that's important, let me explain why it can't be the be-all, end-all.

I was in sixth grade at a public middle school during my parent's ugly divorce, and I was struggling. I had no friends and hated going to school. One day, my mom got a call from my best friend's dad and shared that someone had offered to pay for me to attend a private Christian school. For the next seven years, this anonymous person paid my entire school tuition. I still have no idea who it was, but they obviously impacted me in ways that I will never be able to express.

Now, if you read the chapter for parents (ahem . . . you should!), you are already familiar with my best friend's dad and how truly wonderful he is. While Mr. O wasn't the person who covered my tuition, he was more than just the messenger to my mom. In fact, as I stated in the section to dads, he was truly one of the most intentional people in my life who simply made himself available to me when I needed a friend, a "dad," a financial coach, a spiritual leader, or a car expert. There wasn't one single event that left me so incredibly impressed with Mr. O. It was *years* of small moments of intentionality and relational availability that still make him one of the most important people in my life.

Both the anonymous donor and Mr. O had a significant impact on my life, but I'd only call one of those people today to ask a hard question or share a significant prayer request. Relational availability is more than money and big events and flashy things. You don't need to pay someone's tuition or even be a weekly Bible study leader to do girls ministry. You only need to take what God has given you and be obedient in it.

Are you familiar with the parable of the talents? Essentially, it's a story Jesus tells about a man who entrusts his three servants with money in different yet significant amounts. Let's read the passage below from Matthew 25:14-18 to see how the individual servants handled what their master entrusted them with.

> "For it is just like a man about to go on a journey. He called his own servants and entrusted his possessions to them. To one he gave five talents, to another two talents, and to another one talent, depending on each one's ability. Then he went on a journey. Immediately the man who had received five talents went, put them to work, and earned five more. In the same way the man with two earned two more. But the man who had received one talent went off, dug a hole in the ground, and hid his master's money."

Not going to lie, I would be more than a tad bit jealous if I had been the servant who got the least amount of money. And honestly, it seems like he was just playing it safe and trying not to lose the "little" he had, right? Unfortunately, that is not what the master had in mind. Let's keep reading with verses 19-28.

> "After a long time the master of those servants came and settled accounts with them. The man who had received five talents approached, presented five more talents, and said, 'Master, you gave me five talents. See, I've earned five more talents.' His master said to him, 'Well done, good and faithful servant! You were faithful over a few things; I will put you in charge of many things. Share your master's joy.' The man with two talents also approached. He said, 'Master, you gave me two talents. See, I've earned two more talents.' His master said to him, 'Well done, good and faithful servant! You were faithful over a few things; I will put you in charge of many things. Share your master's joy.' The man who had received one talent also approached and said, 'Master, I know you. You're a harsh man, reaping where you haven't sown and gathering where you haven't scattered seed. So I was afraid and went off and hid your talent in the ground. See, you have what is yours.' His master replied to him, 'You evil, lazy servant! If you knew that I reap where I haven't sown and gather where I haven't scattered, then you should have deposited my money with the bankers, and I would have received my money back with interest when I returned. So take the talent from him and give it to the one who has ten talents.'"

Ouch.

So here we have three servants—two were faithful, one wasn't. The one who wasn't faithful with what the master gave him simply hid his talent. He did nothing with it.

Listen, I am not here to tell you how God is asking you to be relationally available to the teen girls in your life. I don't know them. I don't know what they need, and I don't know what they care about. But I do know that you can't do nothing.

While you could probably use this Scripture to only talk about money, the lesson here for me is that we are to be good stewards of what God has given us. And God has given you something significant to be intentional with. This is not the time for passivity or carelessness.

Did you catch the unfaithful servant's excuse for doing nothing? He was afraid. I'm sure that many of you are fearful of what it might cost you to make yourselves available for the sake of discipleship. I know it can be scary to be obedient to what God calls you to do and what others might think. You might have to sacrifice some things in your life. You might have to rearrange your schedule or give up some convenience once a week. You might do all of that and still be rejected by a teen girl, or she may refuse to believe God could love her.

It *is* scary, but our fear must not be in what we might lose here on this earth or what we might never see the fruit of. Our fear should be directed toward our Master who has entrusted us to love, lead, and disciple His image bearers.

Allow your fear of a holy God to compel you toward relational availability. Take what He has given you—your time, your talents, your money, your passions—and be faithfully obedient with it all. It doesn't matter what fruit you might or might not see from your obedience because what He has given you is already His. It's ultimately His work. He just needs a servant's heart to be surrendered to it.

IT DOESN'T MATTER WHAT FRUIT YOU MIGHT OR MIGHT NOT SEE FROM YOUR OBEDIENCE BECAUSE WHAT HE HAS GIVEN YOU IS ALREADY HIS. IT'S ULTIMATELY HIS WORK.

GET

WHAT SEPARATES
ORDINARY
MOMENTS FROM
TRANSFORMATIVE
MOMENTS IS YOUR
INTENTIONALITY.

CHAPTER 11

PRACTICAL

Regina Barnes has been one of the most important people in my life. She's probably going to kill me when she finds out I'm writing about her, but almost everything I've learned about ministry began with her. It started in 2015 when she rescued me from making popcorn and hot dogs for minimum wage and gave me a job keeping score for men's softball and refereeing kindergarten basketball. It makes me laugh out loud remembering that I first began working in recreation ministry because I do not have a single athletic bone in my body. However, Regina somehow saw my potential and poured into me for over seven years. To this day, I can honestly say that I've never met a more intentional human being than Regina. Everything she does is with purpose, and everything she does is to serve others in a genuine and fun way.

In college, Regina and I had the great idea to participate in the Krispy Kreme Challenge. You run 2.5 miles, eat a dozen donuts, then run 2.5 miles. Sounded like a good time because I do love donuts, but remember me saying I'm not athletic? Well, all I can remember is Regina and her husband practically dragging me over the finish line. We got to mile four, and I was crying, "Just leave me and go!" But I remember Regina grabbing me and yelling, "No, we don't leave family behind!"

PHOTOGRAPHIC EVIDENCE THAT I DID IN FACT RUN A RACE WITH DONUTS. DID I ACTUALLY EAT THE WHOLE DOZEN? I'LL NEVER TELL.

CLEARLY, REGINA AND I NEVER HAD ANY FUN.

Regina never left me behind. She always set me up for success and cheered me on when I felt scared. She always kept it real and honest. She always listened to my rants. And she always made me want to work harder, be better, and love Jesus more every moment that I spent with her. Regina was so intentional, and while she'd never call herself a girls minister, she was the best girls minister I ever had.

There is already so much that you do with your teen girls, but what separates ordinary moments from transformative moments is your intentionality. Whether you're coaching a team, leading a Bible study, mentoring a group of girls, or running a Krispy Kreme Challenge, you can't just go through the motions and expect discipleship to happen. There must be meaningful thought into what you're doing and why you're doing it.

So, let's get practical about how to be intentional in the everyday and weekly moments of girls ministry. In the following sections, I've asked questions that will help you think through some of your ministry methods and evaluate how you can be more intentional in each of these areas.

INTENTIONAL TEACHING

What opportunities do you have to teach your teen girls?

What is your preferred method of teaching?

How do you prepare to teach? What resources do you use?

Who else can speak into what you're teaching teen girls?

What topics are teen girls asking to learn about? What topics do they need to learn about?

How can you do a better job incorporating discussion into your teaching?

INTENTIONAL LEADING

What does it look like for your teen girls to lead?

How do you struggle with releasing control in that area?

_____

_____

_____

How can you give the teen girls in your life more ownership over their own spiritual growth?

_____

_____

_____

INTENTIONAL OUTREACH

What are some of the natural gifts that you see in your teen girls?

_____

_____

_____

How are you equipping them to use those gifts to serve god and serve others?

_____

_____

_____

How are you encouraging them to live on mission locally?

_____

_____

_____

How are you encouraging them to live on mission globally?

If you were to ask your teen girls to share the gospel, could they do it? If not, why?

INTENTIONAL COMMUNITY

How do you encourage community with other believers (young and old) for your teen girls?

Are there other Christian adults engaging in their life? If not, who could you reach out to about this?

GIRLS MINISTRY ISN'T JUST THE FUN EVENTS OR THE MOMENTS WHERE A BIBLICAL TRUTH CLICKS FOR A GIRL. GIRLS MINISTRY IS ABOUT BEING WILLING TO WALK TEEN GIRLS THROUGH BOTH THE MOUNTAINTOP AND VALLEY MOMENTS OF FOLLOWING AFTER JESUS.

COME

CHAPTER 12

READY!

I often talk to my small group girls about the importance of memorizing Scripture. I learned most of my memory verses before even entering high school, yet the years of practice and reading Scripture still allow me to recall Bible verses over fifteen years later. I try to explain to my girls that memorizing Scripture is not really for today (even though it can be). It's for the moments to come when you are faced with temptation or trial, and you need to be reminded of God's Word without even opening it. It's for the times when you feel numb, but God's Word is there to breathe life into your weary soul. Scripture memory is a discipline we put into place for the long-term benefits. And we must discipline and prepare ourselves today if we want to effectively minister and parent teen girls for the long run.

Unfortunately, there is no book or sermon or podcast that can fully prepare you for the challenging moments that come with raising, leading, and loving teen girls. There will be conversations that you won't know how to navigate, and there will be prayers you never thought you'd have to pray. However, we pray, read, and study today to navigate what lies ahead with surrendered hearts and a confidence in the God who goes before us.

I know many of you are thinking, *what's to come? I'm reading this book because nothing prepared me for what I am dealing with right now today!*

Friend, I see you. I see your discouraged or confused heart. You are not alone in your questioning of what to do and how to handle what's in front of you. Take a deep breath and remember this: if you have God's Word in front of you, the Holy Spirit living inside of you, and godly counsel around you, then you are fully equipped to navigate whatever it might be.

We are going to address many of the tough challenges of girls ministry, but there are two questions we must first answer: why do we have hard conversations, and how do we have hard conversations?

Let's start with the first question: Why do we have hard conversations?

No one wants to have hard conversations! I don't think any of us go looking for or running toward confrontation. We aren't laying in bed at night pondering what kind of tension we can stir up the next day. But the reality is that we live in a fallen world, and we are going to face difficult moments with our teen girls. They are going to struggle with sin, and they are going to feel the weight of this broken world.

How horrible would it be for us to pretend that struggles aren't a reality for these girls? To wish them good luck or pass on a "praying for you" comment, but do nothing else to help point them to Jesus in their struggles?

Girls ministry isn't just fun events or moments when a biblical truth clicks for a girl. Girls ministry is about being willing to walk teen girls through both the mountaintop and valley moments of following after Jesus. It's about rejoicing with them when they rejoice and mourning with them when they mourn. It's about celebrating the victories and calling out the sinful patterns. It's about showing up when it's easy and when she doesn't even want you there.

IF YOU HAVE GOD'S WORD IN FRONT OF YOU, THE HOLY SPIRIT LIVING INSIDE OF YOU, AND GODLY COUNSEL AROUND YOU THEN YOU ARE FULLY EQUIPPED TO NAVIGATE WHATEVER IT MIGHT BE.

We don't have a hard conversations to be the rescuer or savior for our girls, but to point them to the One who saves and redeems and restores. You are not the Holy Spirit in these girls' lives, but you do have the power of the Holy Spirit living inside. Therefore, as the Holy Spirit guides you, speak truth and life and wisdom to these girls you have been entrusted with.

Second, how do we have hard conversations?

I like to divide this answer into three steps: listen & watch, love, and respond. You can't do one step without the other two.

LISTEN & WATCH

I am naturally a fixer and a helper. When someone is in need, I am already thinking of ways I can swoop in to deliver a solution. And when it's someone I deeply love or care about, that desire only multiples by a thousand. However, James 1:19 doesn't tell us to be quick to fix, help, or give advice. What does it say?

> "My dear brothers and sisters, understand this: Everyone should be quick to listen, slow to speak, and slow to anger . . ."

When a hard conversation is needed, the first step is to make sure you are actively listening. Are you hearing what she's saying? Do you see where she's struggling? Can you pick out the pain points for her? How is she asking for help?

The goal of listening is to make your teen girl feel known and seen. If you aren't listening before you speak, the way you attempt to love and respond won't translate well.

If you remember Hannah's story (p. 80), you'll remember that Hannah didn't talk much. Listening doesn't always mean sitting while they talk. Teen girls can silently ask for help in numerous ways. Therefore, keep your eyes open. Be watching and waiting and walking with the girls even before they're ready to deal with the stuff happening beneath the surface.

LOVE

Love is the key needed to transition from listening to responding well. We make girls feel heard when we listen, but we must assure them of our love before we ever respond. And not just in the words we say but in our actions too.

The best way we can show Jesus during a hard conversation is not in the advice we give, but the love of Jesus that we get to display. This is the part that humbles us because loving others when it's difficult reminds us of the great love God has shown in our own lives. "But God proves his own love for us in that while we were still sinners, Christ died for us" (Rom. 5:8). Therefore, "We love because he first loved us" (1 John 4:19).

Often, these conversations can entice us to act out of anger or frustration or judgment. It's hard to show love when we are watching our girls make bad decisions and fall into patterns of sin. But to feel safe to share, girls need to know that they can be vulnerable about struggles with empathy and compassion. They must know that our love for them isn't based on their behavior or choices.

 RESPOND

As teen girls feel seen and loved, this is when we lead them out of darkness to show them how to experience healing through Jesus. Our culture, especially among teens, has a hard time receiving truth. Expressions like "your truth is your truth," "you do you," or "whatever feels good" are what they want to hear. It feels like a loving way to respond, right?

But the most loving thing we can do is speak truth: "But speaking the truth in love, let us grow in every way into him who is the head—Christ" (Eph. 4:15). You can't just love them where they are. You need to teach truth in order that they might see the beautiful reality of what it looks like to follow Jesus.

Every situation, struggle, and girl will require a different response from you. Some things require prayer and more time in God's Word. Other times, teen girls may need professional counseling and someone to walk with them through years of healing. This is when you have to rely on the Holy Spirit inside and turn toward godly counsel for the wisdom to know exactly how to respond.

It's okay to admit when you don't know how to handle certain situations, but God will never leave you to do nothing or to stay silent while she continues to suffer or fall into sin. You might have to do some research to find the best response or speak with someone professionally equipped to handle these situations. If you're not sure who to talk to, begin with the ministry leaders at your church.

A few notes of caution here:

1. This is not the chance for you to turn your teen girl's situation into a gossip fest with other friends or even the staff at church. Use wisdom when deciding who to seek for advice in these situations. You can quickly lose a teen girl's trust this way causing even more harm.

2. Your church staff most likely has guidelines in place to respond to certain issues like abuse, self-harm, and so on. This is for the good and protection of the teen girls, as well as the church as a whole. Seek counsel from your church staff if there are any questions about how to properly respond to a situation.

3. If you are having an event with many teen girls, it would be wise to have a licensed counselor on site for questions and issues that might arise.

I can't cover every response to every situation you might face, and I am honestly not qualified to give you the exact steps. However, I've created an exercise to prepare you to handle hard conversations. The chart on the next page will prompt you to fill in the spaces tackling each topic based on our three steps. I've completed the first one to give you some direction on how to fill in the chart on your own. However, this is where your own research and preparation must come into play.

RELY ON THE HOLY SPIRIT INSIDE OF YOU AND TURN TOWARD GODLY COUNSEL TO HAVE THE WISDOM TO KNOW EXACTLY HOW TO RESPOND.

Begin by talking with your ministry leaders about your church's policies on these subjects. From there, work with local counseling offices to create the foundation for these hard conversations, then verify with local law about reporting. Most of these subjects will require help from psychological and counseling professionals, which are usually best found by word of mouth. However, if you need a place to start your search, check out aacc.net (American Association of Christian Counselors).

I've left you a few blanks to add in your own topics. This may be something you're facing today or something you expect will come. The benefit of this exercise is that you have a foundation on which to approach sensitive subjects with caution and wisdom. And all the work you're putting in this exercise will be a game-changer in the way you minister to teen girls and deal with difficult situations.

	LISTEN & WATCH	LOVE	RESPOND
ABUSE	IS SHE SAFE NOW? HOW IS SHE SAFE? WHO HURT HER? WHEN DID SHE GET HURT?	HOW DOES SHE KNOW SHE IS SAFE WITH ME? WHAT IS HER VIEW OF GOD'S LOVE FOR HER?	HOW AND TO WHOM DO I REPORT ABUSE IMMEDIATELY? WHO ELSE NEEDS TO KNOW? HOW DO I GET HER TO SAFETY? HOW DO WE HOPE IN GOD'S FUTURE JUSTICE?
PORN & SEXUAL SIN			
GENDER IDENTITY			

DIVORCE & BROKEN HOME			
ANXIETY & DEPRESSION			
EATING DISORDERS			
SELF-HARM			

One final note: If your church does not have one, create a sheet that includes a list of recommended therapists, as well as hot-line phone numbers for crises. If a teen has a plan to end her life and is not safe, the parents need to be contacted, and they need to seek professional help immediately by going to the ER or calling Mobile Crisis for their area.

HAVE

FUN BREAKS
DOWN THE
SUPERFICIAL
WALLS THAT
TEEN GIRLS
PUT UP.

CHAPTER 13

FUN

If my Sunday school teachers taught me anything, it's that following Jesus isn't boring. These women and their families loved Jesus, and they had fun living a life all about Him. It's what made me want to keep following Jesus even after I graduated, and it's what made me feel like I could love Jesus without giving up a life of fun that our culture promised I would lose.

In all of my years of girls ministry, one of the biggest lessons I've learned is that fun leads to deeper relationships with others and with Jesus. Why do our teen girls love camp and dodgeball nights and girls weekend events? Because they get to hang with their friends! This isn't a bad thing. We want girls to have community with other teen girls who desire to follow Jesus. Community isn't a circle drawn around each individual small group. Community is found when girls recognize all they have in common, and fun is a great way to make that happen.

Listen, I personally want friends that I can study God's Word with and who will hold me accountable. However, I am way more likely to do the first two things if they're the same friends who will die laughing with me when I accidentally say, "Krispy Kreme beans," instead of "crispy green beans." Why? Because they know me, and they love me. They are real life friends, not just "spiritual" friends. That is not me saying fun is a replacement for biblical truth or spiritual depth. It's not. But for many, it is the means to receive it.

Fun breaks down the superficial walls that teen girls put up with one another. They are able get honest about what it looks like to actually follow Jesus in their everyday lives. Fun also allows teen girls to see that parents and leaders fully enjoy living a life surrendered to Jesus.

So, how do we have fun? Well, the possibilities are truly endless! However, I want to give you four basic categories to build a fun foundation with your daughter or group of teen girls: icebreakers, small events, big events, and sneaky Jesus moments. Feel free to use this chapter as a reference guide to keep coming back to time and time again for fresh inspiration on how to incorporate fun into your relationships with teen girls.

ICEBREAKERS

There is nothing more awkward than sitting in a new Bible study group with girls who don't know each other, yet expecting everyone to share deep, personal confessions. From experience, I can tell you that they're not going to do it. It's weird because they're not sure if they can trust you or the situation. However, taking a few minutes at the beginning to ask a fun question or play a game can be the exact thing you need to help girls ready their hearts for a deeper conversation.

Depending on the situation and group size, use one of these icebreaker methods to begin your time with some simple fun.

1. QUESTIONS
You can easily search "conversation starters" online and come up with one or two fun questions to help girls get to know each other. This involves little planning from you, and it is a fun way for girls to learn more about you and what they have in common with the other girls in the group.

FUN BREAKS DOWN THE SUPERFICIAL WALLS THAT TEEN GIRLS PUT UP WITH ONE ANOTHER.

2. GAMES

As I would say in my camp days, recreation rocks the nation! A small stage game, a team-building game, or a large group game can allow teen girls to see their fun, competitive, and creative personalities come to life. If you're not sure what games your teen girls would enjoy, ask them. They might not be into minute-to-win-it style games, but they might surprisingly love dodgeball or a game of spoons.

3. SNACKS & HANGS

There is something so fun that happens when you set out snacks and offer teen girls the chance to hang out with you and each other. I feel like the best conversations often happen in these settings. So pick a snack they love or set an intentional meal for them to enjoy, then allow the chatter to begin and the relationships to form with no obligations besides snacking and hanging.

LARGE EVENTS

There are several large events that commonly happen inside many student ministries: camp, retreats, and Disciple Now. Some might even get to see a girls ministry event hit the calendar two or three times a year. These events often serve two purposes: 1) outreach and 2) intentional growth. They are great for engaging new students and pouring into those who are already involved.

How do we make these large events more fun for our girls, so they desire to go and invite friends to come with them?

1. SHOW UP

We need parents, leaders, and volunteers to show up for these events! The people who are already engaging teen girls year round are the best people to bring the fun because they already know their girls. These large events aren't a replacement for year-round discipleship, but they are an incredible way to build deeper relationships.

HERE IS MY FACE GOING PAINT BALLING AT STUDENT CAMP IN 2021.

And if you can't do something or be somewhere, do whatever you can to make your presence known. Write notes, send a care package, or print a large picture of your face and let your girls take it with them. It's a fun way to show up for them even when you aren't physically there.

2. BE YOURSELF, BUT ALSO BE SILLY

This is a fun way for girls to get to know you. Not as a mom or dad or small group leader, but just you. And you'll get to see them without all the usual distractions. So be yourself, but also have fun! Wear the tutu and the crazy costumes. Jump around with them during worship, get in the mud, and stay up late. The more fun you're having, the more fun your girls are having too.

SMALL MOMENTS

How can you connect with girls one-on-one or in smaller groups? By creating smaller moments of fun. Let's talk about how we can do that.

1. INVITE THEM INTO YOUR DAILY RHYTHMS

Remember those car rides Karis and I took every week? It was something I was already doing that deepened into a discipleship moment. And in this season of life, that's one of the easiest ways for me to connect with teen girls: intentionally inviting them into my normal rhythms of life. I'll text my discipleship group telling them what coffee shop I'm working at and inviting them to join me with their homework, or I'll invite some girls on an errand to Target. I'll even invite them to sit with me in the service on Sunday.

None of that is fancy, but it's an invitation for them to see and experience my life without an agenda or obligation. This is how I connect with the girls intentionally and often where they feel the most comfortable to speak freely.

2. BREAK UP THE ROUTINE

It's easy to get stuck in a routine. Maybe you take your daughter to school at the same time everyday, or you have been leading a small group on Sunday mornings for years. When we (us and our girls) get into a routine, we forget how special these moments really are. Let me encourage you to find ways to break out of your normal routines in order to breathe life into your relationship with your teen girl(s).

This might look like taking her to get coffee on the way to school or getting her out early for a girls trip to get your nails done. This could look like meeting in a different spot for Bible study and bringing homemade cinnamon rolls to group. These once-in-awhile, fun surprises are a great way to take advantage of the small moments and provide an easy way for your teen girl(s) to feel loved.

3. CREATE MEANINGFUL MEMORIES
This is definitely a weakness for me. The creativity of some girls ministers would simply blow your mind. A movie night sitting on pool rafts and watching *The Little Mermaid*? Count me in!

It might look like a Pinterest-worthy activity, or it could just be going for a hike together. Maybe you take her on a trip to celebrate her upcoming graduation or birthday. Maybe you surprise your daughter with a fancy dinner date out with her friends. You know what the teen girls in your life love to do. (If not, ask them!)

These memories are often what outlives anything we teach our girls. However, these memories are deeply tied to what we teach them and how we love them.

SNEAKY JESUS MOMENTS

I had a circle of incredible friends when I was a sophomore in college, and they were the best gift givers of all time. We were constantly looking out for one another, and we always tried to find ways to encourage each other. You never knew when you'd open your front door, or walk out to your car, or show up at church to find a surprise. We eventually called this method of gift giving our "Sneaky Jesus." They were "sneaky" ways to show people Jesus.

Many of the ideas that I use for my girls today started with those friends back in college, which goes to show that simple, intentional gifts are timeless. It's not about what's cool or how much something costs but the thoughtfulness behind the gift. That sounds cheesy, but it is so true. Teen girls just want to know that you care about them, so take the pressure off yourself. You don't need to go big and fancy to make teen girls feel loved or to bring them joy. Just find sneaky or intentional ways to show them the love of Jesus. I promise you'll have a ton of fun doing it.

1. SWEET TREATS

When I couldn't meet with my group of teen girls during COVID, I had a really hard time connecting with them. We would meet over Zoom and a handful of girls would show up, but it was a struggle for all of us. Finally, with so few girls showing up on Zoom or texting back, I had to figure out how to let these girls know that I still cared about them. I texted them one morning and said, "Sonic Happy Hour drinks on me! Text me your order and I'll drop it off between 3-4!" And for the first time in weeks, *all* of my girls responded to me.

Maybe it's not a half-off slush, but maybe your girls love coffee or milkshakes from Chick-fil-A. The current rage with some of my teen girls right now is energy drinks. Why? I don't know! But if I can bring one of my girls an Alani to make her whole day, I'm going to do it.

What can you do to show love in a simply way this week?

_____

_____

_____

2. BIBLE VERSE FLIP CARDS

This is one of my favorite ways to bring encouragement to teen girls, while also giving them a tool that equips them for much longer than a single day. When I have a girl tell me she is struggling with anxiety or stressed about an upcoming test, I love to give them a flip card ring of Bible verses. This gift does several things. It shows that I see the internal battle they are facing. It leads them to actual truth without them having to find it themselves. And it is truth that can be taken with them wherever they go.

All you need to make this gift is a pack of note cards and a loose-leaf ring. Then, you get to pick Bible verses that you think would be the most impactful for the girl and the situation she is walking through. Make sure to write both the Scripture and reference down.

Who do you know that needs a gift like this? What Scripture verses come to mind when you think of her?

3. FLOWERS

Okay, I know not all girls like flowers, but so many do! Flowers can be a thoughtful gift at any time of the year, and while they can feel expensive or fancy, they don't have to be. If you know teen girls who love flowers, I want to share my hack in how to not spend a fortune while using a bouquet of flowers to create a memorable gift.

Purchase some small vases depending on the number of miniature bouquets you'd like to make. You can usually find cheap vases at a discount store, or you can purchase a pack of glass bud vases online for around $20. Once you have your vases, you'll need one medium or large bouquet of flowers (preferably one with greenery included), or you can pick up a couple of value bouquets to make your own assortment.

Open up the bouquet, then begin sorting three to four stems per vase. You can cut the stems to fit the vase, then simply arrange them as desired. You'll see a picture here in the sidebar of some arrangements I made in less than thirty minutes this past Christmas.

Here's a tip for parents: Instead of giving your daughter one vase of flowers for the day, you can decorate her room with all of the small vases or you can surprise her throughout the day with multiple bouquets.

What's an occasion or reason coming up when you can surprise your teen girl or group of girls with flowers?

_____

_____

4. CARE PACKAGES

The first care package I ever received was when I was getting ready to work summer camp and was leaving my friends for ten weeks. I've already told you that they were great gift givers, but they blew it out of the water for this occasion. Not only did they throw me a going away dinner, but they pulled their resources together to shower me with gifts that I could use all summer long. It was a gift that not only showed their support and love, but it was a reminder that I had friends praying for me while I was gone.

This idea is fun for your teen girls, as well. However, consider including her friends or small group in on the idea, too. (If you're a small group or ministry leader, ask parents to contribute!) Create a packing list of what you want to include in the care package, then ask each girl to bring one item. The gift becomes ten times more special because you included the people that love her.

Here's a quick list of ideas for when you might consider making a care package for your teen girl(s): moving away, new driver, birthday, graduation, starting college, sick day, camp, big test day, and salvation decision.

How can you plan a care package for a teen girl or group of girls in the coming month? Who do you want to include?

_____

_____

5. ENCOURAGING NOTES

I am not a sentimental person. I throw away most cards, and I will *not* keep any of my kid's baby teeth—go ahead and judge me. However, in the drawer next to my bed, I have a few cards and letters from my husband. I kept the ones where his words stuck out to me because I needed to hear them more than he even knew as he was writing them.

Our words matter to our teen girls, especially when they're encouraging and uplifting. By taking the time to send a text or write a handwritten note (like the ancient days), you are making her feel so seen and loved. A note and a text are so much more than a passing comment. They are saying, "You mattered enough for me to stop my day to let you know I was thinking about you."

You might choose to write out a long letter of encouragement every now and then. Often, it can be a simply text saying, "Praying for your test this week. You've got this!" Or throwing a sticky note in her car to say that you're proud of her. You might know a big day in her life is coming up, so you plan out multiple notes of encouragement leading up to that day.

What is something you wish your teen girl knew? Why don't you tell her this week?

EXACTLY ONE YEAR AFTER FIRST MEETING TAYLOR, WE TOOK THIS PICTURE BEFORE SHE AND HER TEAM WENT ON TO WIN THAT YEAR'S COLOR WAR.

ALL GIRLS WANT TO HAVE FUN

One of the first times I met Taylor was the night of our big color war event at church. She walked into the church where the rest of the student ministry was decked out in their athletic color apparel as they awaited the paint war that was to come later that night. But Taylor felt like a fish out of water. She didn't know anyone, and she did not want to do anything athletic in front of so many strangers. I'm pretty sure she thought she'd never be back after that night because it was completely out of her comfort zone in every way.

However, her attitude about the church and student ministry changed quickly. To her surprise, I wasn't going to make her participate. Instead of forcing Taylor to run a relay race with a bunch of strangers, I just hung out with her on the sidelines and got to know her. It was the beginning of our friendship, and it was the beginning of her coming to know Jesus.

There's so much of Taylor's story I could tell. When I told her about this book, I asked her what one thing she wanted me to share with the person reading this. And out of all the parts of her testimony I thought she'd want me to include, she instead says, "Tell them to not force someone to participate if it's not in their comfort zone." I kind of laughed at first, but then I realized what she said was so real and so true.

What's fun for one girl might not be fun for everyone. The best game at one church might not be fun at your next. An activity your first daughter loved might be your youngest daughter's worst nightmare.

All girls want to have fun, but it's not going to look the same for everyone. And that's okay! Just like girls ministry isn't a one-size-fits-all, fun isn't either. You have to try different things and be okay admitting when something is a flop.

If you have a group of girls, you also have to be okay not making everyone happy every time you plan something fun. Not everyone wants to make a craft or go pick pumpkins. But do things and invite them to come anyway. If they don't show up, ask what they'd prefer to do next time.

Listen, teen girls are the experts on how they want to have fun. Invite them into the planning process, and let them take the lead on it. This might mean it's less fun for you. (I don't see many dads getting excited to go get pedicures.) However, you want them to be invested in what you're doing together, so let them show you what fun really looks like to them.

After all, girls ministry can't be girls ministry without a ton of fun!

TEEN GIRLS ARE THE EXPERT ON HOW THEY WANT TO HAVE FUN. INVITE THEM INTO THE PLANNING PROCESS AND LET THEM TAKE THE LEAD ON IT!

EVALUATION TOOL: ARE YOU HAVING FUN YET?

Describe the last moment of fun that you planned for your teen girl(s). What was it? How did it go? _____

On a scale of 1-10, how fun was it for your teen girl(s)? _____

On a scale of 1-10, how fun was it for you to plan, prepare, and do it? _____

Why do you think you rated those answers the way you did? What needs to change to see those ratings go up? _____

Did your fun moment include a moment of intentionality? What was the response? _____

Did you hope for a different response? What do you think was the reason for that response? _____

What other people can help you be more thoughtful in your planning and execution of these moments of fun? _____

Name five fun things you want to do this year with your teen girl(s).
1.
2.
3.
4.
5.

Lifeway girls

Helping you point girls to Christ

Social

@lifewaygirls

Blog | girlsministry.lifeway.com

Shop | lifeway.com/girls

Listen | His Glory, Her Good Podcast

additional
resources

SOURCES

Chapter 2

1. "Lexicon, Strong's G4198 - poreuo," *Blue Letter Bible*, accessed February 27, 2023, https://www.blueletterbible.org/lexicon/g4198/esv/tr/0-1/.

2. "C. H. Spurgeon, Witnessing Better than Knowing the Future," *Blue Letter Bible,* accessed February 20, 2023, https://www.blueletterbible.org/Comm/spurgeon_charles/sermons/2330.cfm?a=1019008.

Chapter 3

3. "Most Teenagers Drop Out of Church When They Become Young Adults," *Lifeway Research*, accessed February 20, 2023, https://research.lifeway.com/2019/01/15/most-teenagers-drop-out-of-church-as-young-adults/.

4. "Parents & Churches Can Help Teens Stay in Church," *Lifeway Research*, accessed February 20, 2023, https://research.lifeway.com/2007/08/07/parents-churches-can-help-teens-stay-in-church/.

5. Ibid.

Chapter 4

6. "Reaching Girls Beyond the Church," *Lifeway Girls*, accessed February 20, 2023, https://girlsministry.lifeway.com/2020/01/31/reaching-girls-beyond-the-church/.

7. "Steph Williford of Little Elm, Texas, 1984-2022, Obituary," accessed February 20, 2023, https://www.affoplano.com/obituary/steph-williford?lud=DEDC2D6722965FD4FDEFD92B91171662&fbclid=IwAR18SBCQ8PJOfCSNCZFpAleavsLiLD1YetXvkUbkkclM8flz-yVaC_o2eco.